# eBrandLeaders

## AN INSIGHT INTO 50 OF BRITAIN'S STRONGEST eBRANDS

This book is dedicated to the team – simply for their perseverance and commitment.
Also to the rising brands of the future and to those who have fallen.

Australia • Denmark • Dubai • Holland • Ireland • Philippines • UK • USA

# Marcel Knobil

Chairperson, Superbrands eCouncil
Founder, Superbrands organisation
Chairperson, Creative & Commercial

In a world which is seeing the extinction of internet related companies on a daily basis. Analysts have struggled to establish the ingredient for survival. I believe that a chief ingredient is prudent branding. The best-built ebrands stand the best chance of survival. The following pages explore 50 examples of strong brands that are elevating themselves above the competition.

The eBrandLeaders book is published by the Superbrands organisation – the independent authority on branding. The organisation promotes the discipline of branding and pays tribute to exceptional brands.

The organisation is privileged to have both a Consumer Superbrands Council and a Business Superbrands Council made up of many of the most respected figures in the world of branding. These individuals are responsible for evaluating over a thousand brands and identifying which merit Superbrand status.

There are only a handful of internet-dedicated brands that merit Superbrand status, but there are a number of companies that are building brands in a far superior fashion than the rest of those within the ebrand stampede. The Superbrands eCouncil, made up of eminent figures in the world of internet branding, was established to identify the strongest internet-dedicated brands present in Britain. These brands earn eBrandLeader status.

eBrandLeaders are defined as 'brands which are exclusively dedicated to internet related activity. They have elevated themselves above most other ebrands through offering emotional and/or physical advantages which (consciously or sub-consciously) a critical mass of people, want, recognise, and choose over alternatives on offer'.

Internet sites that capitalise upon existing non-internet related brand status (eg tesco.com and virgin.com) are not considered as candidates for eBrandLeaders. It is the intention that the eBrandLeaders book focuses upon brands that only exist as a result of the internet.

EDITOR-IN-CHIEF
Marcel Knobil

AUTHORS
James Curtis
Jane Simms

MANAGING EDITOR
Blair Hamilford

EDITOR
Angela Pumphrey

ART DIRECTOR
Adam Selwyn

DESIGNER
Maya Twersky

Special thanks to:
Bill Colegrave, Director; Richard Thomas, Director; Annie Richardson, Brand Liaison Director and the Superbrands organisation.

The internet brands scored were identified through many sources. A primary one being, ACNeilsen eRatings.com, to whom we would like to express our gratitude.

ACNielsen eRatings.com is a venture between ACNielsen and NetRatings Inc. ACNielsen, a VNU company, is the world's leading market research firm, offering measurement and analysis of marketplace dynamics, consumer attitudes and behaviour, and new and traditional media in more than 100 countries. NetRatings is the leading provider of Internet audience measurement technology and analysis. Through the Nielsen//NetRatings service, ACNielsen eRatings.com is creating the first global service for tracking audiences, advertising and user activity on the Internet in more than 30 countries worldwide.

Many thanks to Mintel for assisting with research. Mintel defines the consumer marketplace, monitoring product development and providing an important benchmark for future industry growth.

For Superbrands publications dedicated to business-to-business brands, consumer brands and international editions for Australia, Denmark, Dubai, Holland, Ireland, Philippines and USA email: brands@superbrands.org or telephone 020 7267 8899.

Published by Superbrands Ltd
64 West Yard
Camden Lock Place
London
NW1 8AF
www.superbrands.org

Printed in Italy by Printer Trento S.r.l.

ISBN 0-9528153-7-0

# Contents

# Internet Branding

## Why Strong Branding is Critical for Internet-Dedicated Brands
### according to members of the Superbrands eCouncil

**Mike Beeston**

Former Managing Director
Razorfish

The internet invites us to engage with brands. We meet the brand through the logo, design, content, layout, and functionality and respond there and then by clicking and using the brand. We attribute value to this engagement.

At a high level this is true of all brands. On the one hand the brand communication makes a promise to which we relate and the product then delivers. The two are interdependent but distinct. But on the internet the promise and delivery happen together in real time. The brand is inseparable from interaction. On the internet the brand is the brand in action.

Get it right by ensuring that promise and delivery work well together, and you will create a compelling user experience of real value to both brand and consumer. If the promise is less than exciting or, even worse, you fail to deliver, then users will click out for a long time to come. This is brutal. There is no forgiveness. Most get it wrong and don't attract repeat visits. A few get it right and they have a powerful claim amongst users. The internet is not an easy ride but get it right and the world of G3 and interactive TV by comparison will be a doddle.

**Mike Butcher**

News Editor
The Industry Standard

It's difficult to know whether there really is such a thing as an internet brand. The closest you might get could be an Internet Service Provider. All the trends point towards the lines between internet and non-internet companies blurring beyond recognition. What can be said is that websites and their ability to deliver goods or services really IS their brand. If you can't deliver the required customer experience with a well designed site, an information service or physical item then, well, you won't have a brand at all, internet or not.

**Charles Dobres**

Chief Executive
i-Level

Branding is a luxury. That is still the attitude of the vast majority of dotcom and internet-based entrepreneurs. Companies that are built-to-list rather than built-to-last have been slugging it out in a frenzied land grab for new customers and market share. Their sole focus has been on immediate customer acquisition with barely a nod to customer retention and the notion of fundamental marketing practices such as increasing product usage by existing customers. Add to this the fact that dotcoms have no physical high street presence, and therefore no constant awareness builder, and the need for building a brand alongside direct response becomes clear.

Building a strong brand is vital for attracting new customers in the online arena where product comparison is so easy and basic features such as price and specification quickly become commodtised. But brand is equally key in building loyalty and creating further sales from existing customers. Brand building is just delayed-action direct response, so why ignore it?

**Tim Duffy**

Managing Director
M&C Saatchi

A trendy name and a weird advertising campaign do not make a strong brand. Brands are not created magically from scratch. They evolve. And only the fittest will survive the ruthless forces of 'marketing darwinism.'

This is not easy. ebusinesses need an appeal that is magnetic enough to attract customers, but honest enough to retain them. Good branding cannot mask a bad idea nor insure against customer dissatisfaction.

The strongest brands in the virtual world will have extraordinary value. They will be the ones where business and brand grow together to be inseparable. The brand makes a promise and the business delivers. For these companies branding is a way of life.

**Alastair Duncan**

**Managing Director**
**Zentropy Partners UK Ltd**

Brands make promises, ebrands have to prove them.

Strong brands live in the hearts and minds of consumers, remaining true and consistent to a set of values, distilled into words like warmth, trust, or engineering integrity and so on. They remind consumers of these through creative content in distributed technology ie. ads on radio, television or in print, and provide products that people want and enjoy, like great tasting ketchup or meatier burgers. The products themselves prove the advertising promise, and Superbrands, of course, do this best. eBrandLeaders have a different challenge. The medium becomes the brand, and user experience describes how consumers begin to build a relationship, or otherwise, with the brand. Values like engineering integrity or easy ordering ring less true when the site takes four hours to download or there's no space to put your postcode. The best ebrands understand this, and deliver valued information and service in a digestible, organised, usable and enjoyable fashion.

**Scott Gustlin**

**Vice President of European Operations**
**AGENCY.COM**

It is no surprise that strong branding may be the best way to attract and hold customers in the developing internet environment. It is a tough environment defined by the massive proliferation of information, products and services coupled with the ease with which users can move from one site to another. In the rush to achieve the benefits afforded by strong branding, however, many companies have lost the plot. Recent history is littered with examples of companies that have tried and failed to develop brands before, or even independently of, their products or services. While the internet and other digital channels provide new dimensions in which brands must operate, the basic tenants remain the same. The nucleus of a strong brand is the positive experience one consistently has with a company's products, services and people. Winning ebrands build, extend, or reinforce this experience with the use of internet technologies.

**Marcel Knobil**

**Chairperson, Superbrands eCouncil**
**Founder, Superbrands organisation**

Most internet-dedicated brands do not greet us on the shelves of stores, they do not drive past us in the street and we do not see our friends wearing them. We rarely stumble across a site or an engine, we need to be aware of it first. Strong branding results in awareness – an umbilical cord for the survival of many internet dedicated brands. Conventional brands have gradually introduced themselves to us over time. Yet we have been confronted by thousands of internet-dedicated brands in an instant. In an extremely crowded market it is crucial for a brand to differentiate itself from others. Strong branding will elevate one brand over others.

Internet-dedicated brands tend to be distant, impersonal entities that we can't touch or speak to. How do they earn our trust? How do they make us feel warmly about them? How do they excite us? Via an excellent product and exceptional branding.

**Tim Ledgard**

**Head of Marketing and Interactive**
**BBC Online**

It has often been shown that the best way to improve brand value is to focus on increasing customer loyalty. Creating a powerful, motivating and relevant consumer promise is an essential prerequisite for success whether by accident or design. The nature of the internet has not changed these basic marketing principles, despite some fairly notable examples where they have been ignored.

In an environment where for the first year new media upstarts have been significantly challenged by the old media brands who are looking to leverage their established and powerful brand equities, the need for strong branding has never been more critical. We must view this imperative not just from our traditional marketing focus to our customers, but also to the financial markets. Due to the rapid change in each businesses ability to raise capital and the collapse in share valuations the strength of a companies brand has had, I would argue, a very highly leveraged linkage to a company's ability to secure future funding. This underpins the importance of successful marketing and the prizes to be won by creating leading brands within the sector.

**Richard Lord**

**Editor**
**Revolution**

Strong branding is important for every business; when a business is based on the internet, and lacks the reassuring physicality of traditional brands, the intangibles of branding become that much more important. A lot of internet-based businesses are very similar. The barriers to entry are lower than anywhere else; its one of the things that makes the medium so exciting. So the competition will always be fierce, and that pushes differentiation by branding to the forefront.

Strong branding springs from people's experiences of using a product or service. On the internet, the myth so far has been that brand values can be dreamt up in a vacuum and built by plastering them all over billboards, irrespective of whether the product or service lives up to the branding promise. The internet forces businesses to put their customers first; the winning internet brands will be those that give those customers a good experience, and base their branding around it.

**Michael Nutley**

**Editor**
**New Media Age**

One of the most significant effects of the internet has been to transfer power from sellers to buyers. By facilitating price comparisons, eliminating the personal aspects of shopping and enabling consumers to move between retailers at the touch of a mouse, the internet has created an environment where customer loyalty counts for almost nothing. However, recent research indicates that this is only the first phase of online behaviour. Once consumers have some experience of e-commerce, other considerations beyond mere price come into play. These include security, reliability and customer service, and it is here that the value of branding reasserts itself. Not only will those companies with strong brands that represent these qualities attract business from the increasingly suspicious e-customer, they will also resist being sucked into competition purely on price, a battle that ultimately will have no winners.

**William Pulver**

**President**
**ACNielsen eRatings.com**

Tesco, Barclays and BBC are great brands that have benefited from generations of nurturing. Yahoo!, Amazon and eBay are equally great internet dedicated brands, but ten years ago most had never heard of them.

We have lived through a decade of branding revolution driven by the internet. At the end of 2001, over 21 million people have access in the UK, spending over five hours per month surfing. When they go online, it may be to search, shop or browse, but it is always a brand name that dictates behaviour. That brand name may be part of a URL or saved in favourites, but either way it involves some sort of memory.

Few barriers to entry exist for brands on the internet. As quickly as some great brands develop, others may fade away. The fundamentals remain the same, good internet dedicated brands will have to be nurtured over generations.

**David Redhill**

**Vice President, Branding and Marcom**
**BEA Systems**

It has been said that the brands we most enthusiastically buy into are those which possess the personality and values we might find in a friend. If so, these 'friends' have traditionally been pretty boring in the way that they relate to us: static, repetitive and unchanging from year to year. With the internet, however, has come the possibility of brand relationships that evolve on a daily basis. By personalising its offer to individual tastes, an online brand really can become someone who knows you, understands your preferences, and tells you something new every time you make contact. In this dynamic state, and with alternatives just a few clicks away, strong branding and the intelligent use of customer information has never been more critical to achieving relevant differentiation, and to building customer loyalty. After all, would you socialise with someone who kept asking you the same questions and continually ignored your replies? Certainly not – and nor would you be loyal to an online brand which did the same.

## Jim Rose

**Chief Executive Officer**
**QXL.com**

Strong branding is critical for internet-dedicated brands and not just for the obvious reasons. The internet – itself a new medium of distribution – brings with it challenges of trust, credibility, security and confidentiality, on top of other brand attributes such as values, loyalty, differentiation and consumer identity. The other challenge of the internet-dedicated brand is that it is virtual in nature and not necessarily attributable to a physical tangible good.
Since the internet brands are virtual by their very nature, strong brand development is essential. The emerging landscape of the internet makes it paramount for brands to be creative when they are being developed, so that they communicate and represent the essence of the internet medium. Customers must be able to identify the positive attributes of the brand. The sooner the trust and confidence is developed in the brand, the quicker the business can accelerate and achieve eBrandLeader status.

## Evan Rudowski

**Managing Director**
**Excite**

Internet brands have two big consumer challenges:
– a plethora of high profile dotcom failures means consumers are sceptical.
– the internet is very functional with low emotional attachment.
Strong branding will build trust and will also ensure consumers know what each brand stands for, which today is a gap as its all classified as 'dotcom'.
Creating a brand personality around distinct and deliverable brand values will also start to grow emotional links. Above all, strong branding will ensure consumers consider internet dedicated brands alongside other strong consumer brands and not just as 'dotcoms' and the baggage that has been created in such a short time.
It will be critical to achieve longevity and stand out in an already cluttered category.

## Felix Velarde

**Chief Executive**
**Head New Media**

The inspiring thing about the web has always been that anyone, really anyone, can set up a web-based venture. And it can cost next to nothing. My first website took me a week. So I can see your (very well funded) idea, copy it at little expense, and make a profit more quickly than you can...
All things being equal, the technology will be functional, I'll get the product I ordered, at the same cost wherever I buy it.
The difference will be in how convenient it was, how quick, intuitive, simple it was. How my problems were dealt with, or how it was shown they would have been. Then deliver. Suddenly I'm having a positive relationship with your brand. Make me associate this positive experience with something that is visually unique. In a crowded, instantly-updated, ephemeral world, you have a strong brand.
You win.

## Dave Wilby

**Technical Editor**
**Internet Magazine**

Strong branding is close to my heart. When we launched in 1994, the publishers followed the 'generic name' strategy. They wanted unmistakable branding for an internet magazine, and plumped for 'Internet Magazine'. A no-brainer tactic which works traditionally (Fruit Pastilles), and virtually (www.weather.com).
The internet is many things: a communications lifeline, blank canvas of innovation, global community of lost souls. But commercially, it is simply a new exploitable medium. Long-term, we will choose internet companies for price, performance and fulfilment. More immediately, building brand is key. The internet remains embryonic. We CAN be the Coca-Cola of our industries. New domains open new opportunities. Lost your dream dotcom brand? What price, your.bank or the.shop? The internet is dynamic, interactive and offers unprecedented opportunities, but some things remain the same. Our companies and URLs leap to mouths and mice, if we produce damn fine products/services at prices that produce smiles. It is the same game.

## Market Context

As the world's population goes online in ever increasing numbers, e-commerce is now emerging as a major economic player in providing goods and services directly to consumers. Alongside this internet revolution there has been a shift from analogue to digital technology within the electronics industry. This new technology has changed the way we run our lives both at home and in the work place. Today the word 'digital' has become synonymous with an up-to-date, high-quality lifestyle.

21store.com is riding the wave of both the e-commerce and digital revolutions. It is predicted that purchasers using the web will increase from 31 million in 1998 to 183 million in 2003 (Source: Forrester Research). In addition, the digital market is set to be one of the most buoyant sectors over the next ten years. For example, 5.4 million palmtop computers (PDAs) were sold in 1999 but it is projected to increase to 18.9 million units by 2003 (Source: IDC) and the sale of digital cameras increased in 2000 by 113% (Source: IDC). While internet users continue to increase and digital product life cycles decrease, as new models outdate their predecessors, 21store.com is provided with a major business opportunity in the marketplace as it grows, recreates and refreshes itself.

21store.com's main competition comes in the form of traditional retailing giants such as Dixons, Comet, Tempo and Jessops, most of which are now developing their own online proposition. Pure play e-tailers, ranging from small specialists such as widget.com and unbeatable.co.uk to larger dotcom companies selling digital products alongside a number of other product categories such as Jungle.com and Buy.com, have also captured a significant share in the market.

Today, 21store.com has secured its position as a major player with established brand values in the rapidly developing digital e-commerce market.

## Achievements

21store.com has a proven five year track record of success as an e-tail concern, which equates to over 21 'internet years' of experience. Since its launch, up to 2000 turnover has doubled each year. Significantly, 21store.com has secured repeat purchases from over 50% of existing customers, and the company continues to expand worldwide; to date making sales in over 58 countries. Its credibility as an established company has secured support from major suppliers of digital products. In addition investment with major blue-chip companies, including The Carphone Warehouse, and partnerships with established dotcoms such as egg.com and beeb.com, all contribute to the company's overall status within the marketplace. Focused marketing activity revolving around extensive PR and advertising both on and offline has proven highly successful; in July 2000 21store.com was rated as the 17th best known e-tailer in the UK (Source: I-recall Survey, Campaign Magazine).

## Key Management

Geoff Brady, Chairman of 21store.com, brings considerable retail experience and success to the business having held senior management positions with blue-chip retailers such as Kingfisher, Sainsbury's and Allied Carpets. Brady's expertise and notable qualities are conveyed through his professionalism

and innovative approach, which have driven 21store.com to the forefront of the e-commerce market.

Prior to becoming a founding member of 21store.com, Michael King, Managing Director, enjoyed a successful career with ICL and Reuters. Since becoming the Managing Director of the company in December 1998, Mike has overseen and played a vital role in 21store.com's continuous growth and expansion.

## Background

21store.com was founded in 1995 as one of the first e-commerce ventures

operating from the UK. Jointly created by Mike King and Louis Berk the company (then known as Business on the Move Ltd) initially negotiated a distributorship for Psion. During 1996 and 1997, when 21store.com was run from a private house in Hertfordshire, a number of significant new products were added to the portfolio including a wider range of handheld computers, Global Positioning Systems and Digital Cameras.

In 1998 a major international initiative was embarked upon with the establishment of 21store.com Inc, a wholly owned subsidiary based in New Hampshire. During this period, rapid growth continued in the UK and 21store.com moved to Wembley where it currently runs its operations in a 5,000 square foot office and distribution centre.

## Product/Service

The 21store.com website currently offers an extensive range of over 900 digital products, such as PDAs, Global Positioning Systems, Digital Cameras, DVDs and other related items, to both the consumer and business markets. Industry leaders such as Psion, Palm, Fujifilm, Casio, Ericsson, Kodak and Garmin feature widely in the product range. The company keeps abreast of constant new product developments in digital and emerging WAP technologies to meet the needs of its core customer base.

21store.com makes customer satisfaction a priority throughout the buying experience. Orders can be processed via the internet, phone, or fax – all three are secure methods of payment – with 90% of customers receiving orders within 24 hours of purchase. 21store.com prides itself on offering prices that are lower than UK high-street competitors and remains competitive with online retailers. Above all, the staff's superior knowledge of digital technology enables them to advise the customer comprehensively and with ease.

The 21store.com website is at the cutting edge of technology and is constantly revised ensuring it meets customers' demands for website service, speed and navigability. 21store.com has expanded its website services to include partnerships with associated companies such as photobox.co.uk, to offer its customers developing and printing of digital photographs.

## Promotion

In March 2000, a marketing programme was launched in the UK alongside a re-branding initiative which was designed to meet several of the company's key objectives including: communication of 21store.com's specialisation in digital products; increasing overall awareness of the 21store.com brand name; and creating sales of 21store.com merchandise.

21store.com reaches its marketing objectives using a combination of both on and offline activity through targeted advertising, extensive PR and the establishment of affiliate partnerships. Targeted to reach a predominantly male audience, product-led branded advertising has focused regionally on London via the Evening Standard and Metro Newspapers, with a wave of advertising reaching a national audience through specialist magazines. A cohesive public relations strategy has been running since November 1999 centred on establishing the 21store.com brand through media relations, product reviews, cyber promotions, competitions, online tracking and speaker platforms. To date coverage has increased by 20% each month securing high quality exposure in specialist publications, national newspapers and broadcast media including BBC Radio and The Big Breakfast. In August 2000, The Times gave 21store.com "8/10 for the site, particularly good customer service" and in February 2000, Computeractive said "If it's boy's toys and gadgets that ring your bell, then you'll love this site." Affiliate marketing has also been an essential promotional tool. Since its launch, the UK marketing campaign has proven highly successful increasing brand awareness and driving sales.

## Brand Values

The chosen name 21store.com reflects the company's recognition of the fundamental importance of digital technology in the twenty first century. 21store.com's tagline 'We Know Digital' encapsulates the reputation and credibility for which the company is renowned. 21store.com continues to pursue its policy of constant improvement in customer care, purchase protection, value for money and technological expertise.

## Future Plans

The digital e-commerce market is constantly evolving and 21store.com is well equipped with the flexibility and experience to thrive in this environment. Future initiatives include the launch of an additional service in the expanding B2B market enabling the fulfilment of large order requests for corporate businesses and government departments. In the worldwide market, the company continues to plan its expansion via selected foreign portals. 21store.com continues to expand its customer service management policies.

**www.21store.com**

# amazon.co.uk™

## Market Context

Consumers have been shopping online for nearly a decade and recently more and more people have embraced e-commerce resulting in an online retail market boom.

Pioneering 'pureplay' operations have developed strong brand identities. More than ever before factors such as outstanding customer service, choice, ease of use and value for money have become the overriding tenets of successful online retailing.

Within this environment Amazon has established itself worldwide as an online retail success. 23 million UK adults use the internet and three million customers have shopped at Amazon.co.uk – nearly one in eight UK internet users have made a purchase at Amazon.co.uk (Source: National Office of Statistics March 2001).

## Achievements

Amazon.co.uk has set the standard for online retail and continues to pioneer the growth and development of e-commerce in the UK. An Interbrand survey in July 2000, named Amazon.com as the 48th most valuable brand in the world.

With over three million customers, Amazon.co.uk is the leading e-commerce site in Europe. It took Amazon.co.uk fifteen months to reach its millionth customer, a further eight months to reach its second million and just six months more to reach its third. Amazon.co.uk and its American counterpart, Amazon.com, are ranked number one and two respectively by Jupiter MMXI's online retailer league excluding shopping comparison sites (February 2001). Amazon have more unique British visitors each month than the next nine most visited online retailers combined.

Internal customer research shows that over 70% of Amazon.co.uk's sales are from repeat customers and that 97% of Amazon.co.uk customers are 'satisfied' or 'very satisfied' with the service they receive from the site.

In April 2001, Amazon.com Inc announced that net sales for the first quarter of 2001 were US$695 million, an increase of 21% over net sales in the first quarter of 2000. The company also expects Amazon.com to reach operating profitability in the fourth quarter of 2001.

At the beginning of 2000, more than one in four UK online purchases were made via Amazon.co.uk – with an estimated one in every two books bought online coming from the site (Source: Fletcher/Forrester UK Internet User Monitor May 2000). Amazon.co.uk is also a significant exporter of UK-originated products, and now has customers in 217 countries worldwide.

In the UK, Amazon.co.uk has won many industry awards including Best Online Retailer in the Revolution Awards, December 2000; Customer Service Visa e-tail Awards January 2001; Made to Measure Visa e-tail Awards January 2001 and Gomez Music Award Autumn 2000.

## Key Management

Jeff Bezos, Founder and Chief Executive Officer, has always been interested in anything that can be revolutionised by computers. Intrigued by the amazing growth in use of the internet, Jeff created a business model that leveraged the internet's unique ability to deliver huge amounts of information rapidly and efficiently. In 1994, he founded Amazon.com Inc an internet retailer of books, music and other information-based products that offered services traditional retailers could not such as lower prices, extensive selection and a wealth of product information.

Diego Piacentini has been Senior Vice President and General Manager International since March 2000. Diego is responsible for overseeing the company's existing international businesses in France, Germany and the UK as well as future global expansions.

Steve Frazier, Managing Director took up his position in January 2000. Steve has overall responsibility for maintaining Amazon.co.uk's market position as the leading online retailer in the UK. This includes expanding the business and ensuring that customers benefit from the best possible online shopping experience.

## Background

Amazon.com opened its virtual doors in July 1995 with a mission to use the internet to transform book buying into a fast, easy and enjoyable shopping experience. While the site's customer base and product offerings have grown considerably since the early days, Amazon still maintains a founding commitment to customer satisfaction and the delivery of an educational and inspiring shopping experience.

Today, Amazon.com offers much more that just books. It has the 'Earth's Biggest Selection™' of products, customers can browse through more than 28 million unique items in categories such as electronics, kitchen products, books, music, DVDs, videos, camera and photo items, toys, software, computer and video games, tools and hardware, lawn and patio items, and wireless products. Through Amazon.com zShops, any business or individual can sell virtually anything to Amazon.com's customers and with Amazon.com Payments sellers can accept credit card transactions, avoiding the inconvenience of offline payments.

## Product/Service

Amazon.co.uk offers more than 2.5 million products and provides a complete online storefront for individual merchants through its zShops. This amounts to almost every UK book in print, three times as many CDs as customers would find in a large high street store and practically every video and DVD available in the UK.

It offers industry-leading, online shopping technology such as secure credit-card payment, personalised recommendations, streamlined, 1-Click® ordering and easy to use Bid-Click auction bidding.

Since Amazon.co.uk customers range from new online shoppers to internet shopping experts, the site is designed to cater for all. The structure of the Amazon.co.uk site allows all customers to flick between different sections (stores) and navigate their way round the site quickly and easily.

Amazon.co.uk's pre-order facility allows customers to order a product before it is released to ensure that as soon as it does become available their copy is posted immediately. Never was this better illustrated than for the publication of Harry Potter and The Goblet of Fire in July 2000 – Amazon.co.uk received over 65,000 pre-orders – one for every 200 children in the UK.

Amazon.co.uk has panels of literary, music, kids and technology experts on board to write reviews of new products. In addition, customers are also invited to give their own personalised reviews of products.

The Amazon.co.uk Associates Programme allows member websites to earn extra money

on every book, CD, video, DVD, software or PC and video game sold through their site. Associates choose products that are of interest to their visitors, add their own reviews and recommendations on the web page and then link directly to their local Amazon catalogue. There are now over 40,000 members in the UK programme and over 600,000 worldwide.

Amazon.co.uk currently exceeds UK government recommendations for security – using up to date SSL technology (shown on site by the reassuring padlock in the bottom right hand corner of the page) and keeping customers informed every step of the way. As the government's new Distance Selling Directive came into force in October 2000, giving more protection to people shopping online, Amazon.co.uk was pleased to announce that it already went beyond these guidelines to keep its customer promises.

In November 2000 Amazon.co.uk's new 46,450 square metre distribution centre opened, with the capacity to ship 100,000 packages an hour at its peak. This is the largest distribution centre in Europe (for an online retailer) and is the size of eight football pitches.

## Promotion

Amazon.co.uk has a comprehensive, integrated marketing strategy that encompasses advertising, public relations, promotions, online marketing and customer relationship marketing. Existing key partners include American Express, Yahoo! and MSN.

## Brand Values

Amazon.co.uk aims to offer the fastest, easiest and most enjoyable shopping experience for UK online customers. While its customer base and product offering have grown considerably since the early days,

Amazon.co.uk maintains its 100% commitment to customer satisfaction and the delivery of an inspiring shopping experience. In 2000 over 99% of packages were shipped to customers before Christmas.

## Future Plans

While details of Amazon's future developments remain commercially sensitive, customers in the UK can be sure that Amazon.co.uk will continue to be much more than a 'dotcom', aiming to offer unrivalled customer service and striving to offer the most exciting, extensive and innovative product line up available from any single retailer.

**www.amazon.co.uk**

## Market Context

This is the internet century and the industry is one of the most competitive, fast growing and fast-paced in the world. A few years ago, relatively few people had heard of the internet, let alone ISPs. Now the internet is big news and plays an important part in people's everyday lives. Indeed, when America Online Inc announced it was to join forces with the media owner Time Warner, it wasn't just something to read about on the business pages but made front page news.

Many ISPs have come and gone and only the strongest survive. Industry leaders will be those who focus on the consumer, providing them with quality, convenient and easy-to-use services that are safe.

## Achievements

From the first service launch in 1995, AOL Europe's multiple brands now reach more than 4.6 million households across Europe. Worldwide, AOL enjoys a membership of more than 30 million.

AOL UK's unique and pioneering Corporate Responsibility Team – believed to be the only one of its type in Europe – focus on extending the benefits of the online medium to those who would most benefit from access but are least likely to obtain this

through traditional means. It is responsible for liaison with UK and European policymakers addressing 'Digital Divide' issues, and for the AOL UK Community Investment programme which supports a range of charities working with children at risk and people with disabilities. The AOL Schools programme enables thousands of UK schools to get online, for the first time.

AOL members in the UK are loyal to the service and spend a lot of time within the content areas of the service rather than on the internet at large. In fact, according to December 2000 MMXI figures, AOL Europe members average 246.3 minutes a month in AOL content areas, more than three times the minutes spent by members in the content areas of the next most popular ISP.

## Key Management

Karen Thomson, Managing Director, AOL UK and Executive Vice President, AOL Europe, is responsible for the management and marketing of the company's three UK brands – AOL, CompuServe and Netscape Online. Appointed to the role in August 1999, Thomson previously served as Executive Vice President of Marketing for AOL Europe and as Marketing Director for AOL UK since its launch in January 1996.

Widely viewed within the internet industry as one of the top marketing professionals, Thomson was responsible for bringing 'Connie, the online genie,' to the UK's TV-watching public.

## Background

Since it was first launched AOL UK has become the UK's leading interactive services company. A division of AOL Europe, AOL UK is committed to the same multiple-brand strategy successfully developed by AOL in the US. Notably, the leading AOL, CompuServe and Netscape Online services, AOL Instant Messenger, as well as, AOL and CompuServe portals in ten countries and five languages across Europe.

On May 26 2000 OFTEL, the UK telecommunications regulator, ended BT's role as gatekeeper to the internet by forcing it to open its networks to competitors. The decision set the stage for full and fair competition among all access providers, providing true unmetered internet connections, while mandating significantly lower costs.

The ruling signalled a victory for consumers, competition and common sense enabling UK consumers to at last benefit from true US-style internet access. For AOL UK the decision was significant and marked the end to its eighteen-month campaign to 'stop the clock' and end metered rates, citing them as the main obstacle to the development of the 'net economy' in the UK.

AOL worked to show that the absence of flat-rate internet telephone access was an issue of critical importance for the future of the UK economy, and should be of concern to OFTEL, the UK telecommunications regulator.

### Product/Service

AOL provides a safe service for the whole family with interactive education, entertainment, financial and information content while giving access to a global online community.

AOL is the largest subscription-based ISP in the UK. The service is user-friendly and is looked upon as an ideal first step onto the internet for the entire family. AOL comprises of eighteen channels of high quality content to suit a wide range of interests. In addition to the channels, AOL includes features such as AOL Parental Controls to ensure children can go online in safety, AOL Instant Messenger, AOL Search, and new with version 6.0, AOL Groups and AOL Calendar. AOL.co.uk is the web portal for non-AOL members. The site reaches a wide audience of internet users and offers a taste of the AOL member experience.

As part of its AOL Anywhere strategy, AOL Europe has announced alliances with technology manufacturers and mobile network operators. These alliances extend AOL's world class content, community and hallmark ease-of-use to mobile platforms.

oriented service, as well as launching new pricing plans and lobbying for industry change.

Summer 2000 proved to be a pivotal time in AOL's marketing history, with the brand launching a number of promotions.

At the Live 2000 exhibition, AOL welcomed thousands of visitors to the 'AOL House', an exhibition covering 367 square metres. It comprised a kitchen, study, living room and kid's playroom, and featured four giant plasma screens and 45 PCs for attendees to try out AOL.

Several joint-marketing initiatives were announced with leading UK bricks and mortar retailers. First of these was the strategic alliance with Carphone Warehouse, for the Mviva independent mobile internet portal. This saw AOL take a 15% stake in Mviva, and its PC-based service promoted in more than 800 Carphone Warehouse and Phone House retail outlets across six European countries.

AOL also linked up with Wal-Mart Europe to cross-market services and brands. The alliance covered the distribution of AOL discs in Wal-Mart's 240-strong chain of ASDA stores.

### Promotion

In 1998 AOL UK broadened consumer reach through the first mainstream television advertising campaign by an internet provider. The pioneering commercials launched 'Connie, the online genie,' who has become an instantly recognisable, interactive icon for the service and its members.

Advertising campaigns continue to promote AOL as a safe, family-

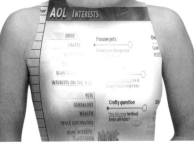

### Brand Values

AOL is the safe internet service for all the family offering up to seven email addresses.

It is designed to be simple for anyone to use, whatever their age and whatever their technical (or non-technical) knowledge and prides itself on being easy-to-use and offering something for everyone.

### Future Plans

In January 2001 AOL and Time Warner completed their merger to create AOL Time Warner Inc. Jerry Levin, Chief Executive Officer of AOL Time Warner said: "AOL Time Warner's scale, scope and reach will enable us to capitalise on the digital revolution that is shaping global media, entertainment and communications on behalf of consumers worldwide."

**www.aol.co.uk**

## Market Context

As the internet continues to explode, it is becoming harder for people to find useful, objective information online. As a result, some of the strongest and best-known internet brands are those which help people find what they are looking for – classically known as search engines.

Many of these search engines rely on a technology called Boolean logic, a system that allows commands to be mapped into bits and bytes, to match keywords with web addresses. But in itself, Boolean logic can be a complicated and frustrating experience for many users, particularly if they are new to the web, because it requires a skill to use the right combination of key words, mathematical symbols and punctuation marks to find things and then there is no guarantee that the results will be relevant.

Ask Jeeves UK (www.ask.co.uk), overcomes these problems because it allows users of any online skill level to ask questions in plain, natural English and directs them to a web page with the relevant answer. The whole look and feel of the service is designed to be friendly and easy to use, literally humanising the internet experience.

## Achievements

Since its launch on February 24th 2000, Ask Jeeves UK has achieved phenomenal success. By April of the same year the service was among the top ten UK favourite websites and its name was among the best known on the web. This was borne out in September 2000 when readers of the UK's most widely read internet magazines voted Ask Jeeves as 'Best Portal' in the Future Publishing Internet Awards. Today, Ask Jeeves UK has a reputation for being one of the first places new users come to find what they want on the web, answering over 900,000 questions each day. In fact by the time Ask Jeeves UK was celebrating its first birthday in February 2001, over 270 million questions had

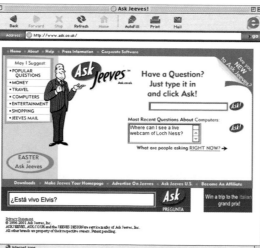

been asked on the site and nearly three billion answers had been returned.

The brand's use of innovative, patented technology to facilitate searching for information on the web is another important achievement. Its unique natural-language question and answer approach to web searching is one of the most sophisticated internet technologies on the market, yet it is easy to use and is constantly helping to open up the net to new and inexperienced users.

## Key Management

The core UK executive management team consists of CEO, George Lichter, Chief Operating Officer, David Gerken and Senior Vice President of Sales and Marketing, Adrian Cox. Reporting into them are the various functional heads of Sales, Marketing & PR, Business Development, Editorial, Finance, IT and Site Engineering.

## Background

Founded in 1996 in Emeryville, California, Ask Jeeves was the brainchild of Garrett Gruener, a venture capitalist and David Warthen, the creator of the Ask Jeeves natural language technology. In April 1997, www.askjeeves.com was launched, fast becoming the leading provider of question and answer services on the web. In 1998, the company launched Ask Jeeves for Kids (www.ajkids.com) – a fun and child-friendly version of the original that allows kids to use the same natural-language approach but with added safety features.

Quickly, Ask Jeeves grew from a small enterprise to an international organisation. In February 2000, Ask Jeeves UK was launched as a joint venture between Ask Jeeves International, Carlton Communications plc and Granada Media Group. Both these media giants became involved in Ask Jeeves UK to reinforce their commitment to exploring opportunities in new media and the company has become an important addition to their respective portfolios.

Towards the end of 2000, Ask Jeeves became the default search facility for users of ONnet, the interactive web service from ONDigital.

### Product/Service

Jeeves can answer questions as simple as 'Where can I find rail timetables?' and 'Where can I buy CDs online?', or more complicated requests such as 'What was the biggest earthquake to ever hit the UK?' and 'Am I in love?'

In order to find the most relevant answer in the most efficient way, ask.co.uk uses a combination of web navigation methods. Firstly, sites are selected by a team of UK editors who apply strict quality controls to pick out only the best sites on the web to answer a user's question. The second method involves Ask Jeeves' unique popularity-based technology, which automatically searches the web and tracks the most popular sites as defined by other users of these sites. Finally Ask Jeeves also uses a 'meta-search' facility to see what relevant sites other search engines such as Lycos, Yahoo! and AltaVista find, giving the user the 'best of the rest' in one go.

Qualitative research regularly undertaken by Ask Jeeves has led to constant refinement of the site, such as introducing a 'new user guide' for first time users which takes people through the ask.co.uk site step by step, and making the 'Ask a question' box a central part of the site. There are also other elements to the Ask Jeeves product, such as Jeeves Mail. Launched in August 2000, this is a free e-mail and calendar service. Another extension to the service was the Ask Jeeves shopping channel, launched in October 2000 which offers twelve product categories and a special seasonal area to help users find just what they are looking to buy.

Ask Jeeves has signed up a number of exclusive partners including eBay, QM4 and DealTime to provide users with more advanced shopping services such as an online auction, request for quote and price comparisons. For added reassurance, all sites chosen in any section of the channel will have undergone a strict selection process to make sure that they offer the best possible shopping experience.

In September 2000 Ask Jeeves introduced a revolutionary new advertising model Dynamic Response Anchor Tenancies (DRATs), allowing advertisers to effectively 'own' key words, so that their ad appears every time their keyword is included in a question. This delivers information about products and services directly to users who have already expressed an interest in that particular area.

### Promotion

With an initial marketing investment of £10 million, Ask Jeeves had a high profile launch in the UK across television, radio, press and online. This was executed through advertising and PR, including nationwide 'Butler Blasts' where actors dressed as butlers went out onto the streets, at train stations, at events such as Wimbledon and in support of Valentines Day to raise awareness of the brand and its associated values.

In October 2000, Ask Jeeves ran a week-long promotion with The Express newspaper to win a life of luxury worth £100,000. During early 2001 a number of smaller promotions ran on the site based around seasonal opportunities such as Valentines Day and Easter.

In April 2001 a new multimillion pound TV campaign was launched which continues the aim to drive people to the site using the proposition that if you have a question, Ask Jeeves. This theme ran through into press ads and an online campaign.

### Brand Values

The personality of the brand, embodied by the character Jeeves, has achieved fame across all media. Now almost a celebrity figure in his own right, Jeeves is the world's first internet butler and is instantly recognisable. Jeeves is efficient, easy to use, reliable, friendly, intelligent, trustworthy and has become synonymous with helping you find what you are looking for on the web.

### Future Plans

During the early months of 2001, Ask Jeeves UK introduced a service called Answerlink. This is where companies whose sites have been deemed relevant as an answer, but where they are displayed as part of a drop-down list of answers, can pay to ensure that they are returned as the default. This does not affect the impartiality of the answers returned as all sites are editorially selected regardless of any commercial arrangements. The service was introduced as part of an ongoing aim to find new and effective ways of monetising its site without compromising the user experience.

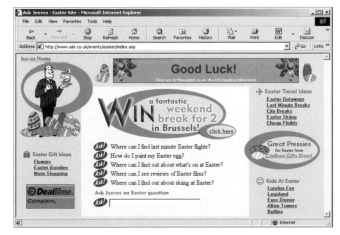

Moving forward, the company will be introducing new site developments and constant refinements to make the ask.co.uk service more intuitive and user-friendly, particularly for new internet users.

**www.ask.co.uk**

# bargainholidays.com

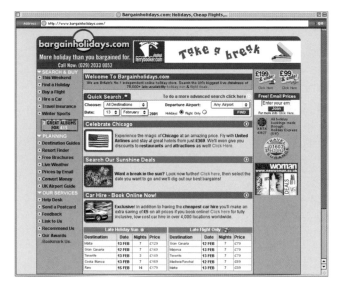

## Market Context

The online travel retail market is currently one of the most competitive commercial sectors within the UK. As users are becoming more familiar and confident with the internet, holidays are increasingly booked online. By providing consumers with quality services that can be tailored to their needs Bargainholidays.com continues to remain among the key players in this sector.

Competitors in the market come in many forms. Increasingly, established tour operators such as Club Med and Kuoni are extending their services into online operations and offering online booking facilities. Airlines such as easyJet offer discounted flights online and are driving down the cost of flights to popular destinations. Competition also comes from other online travel services such as ebookers.com, Expedia.co.uk and Travelocity.com.

## Achievements

Market intelligence suggests that Bargainholidays.com is one of the top three sites in terms of traffic, transactions and users as well as being in the top five for its level of customer awareness.

Named as one of the Top Websites of 1998 by The Guardian, Bargainholidays.com was also a finalist in the 1998 Financial Times Business Website of the Year Awards, the 1998 New Media Age Effectiveness Awards and the Best Commercial Website category of the 1998 Yell UK Web Awards.

Bargainholidays.com was commended in the 2000 New Media Age Effectiveness Awards having been declared in 1999 to be one of The

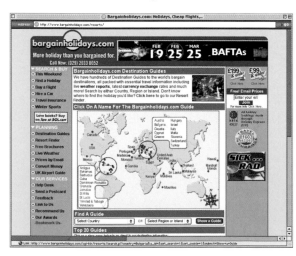

World's Top 300 Internet Sites by PC Magazine. Also that year it was in the finals for an unprecedented two Revolution Magazine New Media Awards as well as being nominated for a 1999 Yell UK Web Award.

The service has also been named a Yahoo! Pick of the Week, AOL Pick of the Week, BBC Web Guide Top Site, Internet Magazine Site of the Month, The Guardian Weekly Web Pick, Sunday Times Travel Site of the Week, The Guardian Top 100 website, EU What's New Site of the Day, Revolution Magazine Top 100 Site, Internet Monthly Top 10 Site, TescoNet '100 Best' Website, BBC TV Really Useful Website, .Net Magazine Top 100 Site, .Net Magazine's PC Advisor Top 50 Essential Selection Site and was rated best holiday site by New Media Age and "quite simply the best place to get yourself a bargain" by Internet Advisor.

## Key Management

Paul Donohue joined Emap in 1999 as Producer of Bargainholidays.com. He has overseen the development and expansion of the site, increasing both traffic and revenue to record levels.

He has also overseen the development of other products for the group including A2bTravel.com and Escaperoutes.com.

Paul previously worked as a television production manager for BBC television's Arena arts series and managed the in-house production company for the Virgin group as well as writing for magazines such as GQ and Boys Toys.

John Bevan, Managing Director, Emap Digital Travel, joined the company as Commercial Director in August 2000, and has brought fourteen years of travel industry experience to Digital Travel. Past experience includes time spent as the International Sales Director for hotel group, Groupe Envergure where responsibilities included a pan-European sales force selling to Tour Operators worldwide.

John also managed the call centre, putting in place a new Automatic Call Distribution System (ACD) and built the specifications for a new reservations programme. He created and launched his own website www.bookthat.com selling Tour Operator villas online.

## Background

Bargainholidays.com, is owned by Emap Online and is one of the UK's longest established online holiday services. Launched in 1997, the concept behind the site was very simple: To offer the widest available choice of late availability package holidays (including flight only deals) at the lowest prices, online, seven days a week. This concept has developed over the years with the site now offering a full travel service that includes everything from travel insurance to online car hire.

## Product/Service

Bargainholidays.com provides its users with a comprehensive travel offer to enable products and services to be sourced from one point. It has about 70,000 holidays displayed on the site at any one time in addition to flight

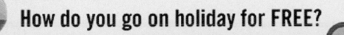

booking engines with versions for both scheduled and charter flights. Visitors can also use a facility on the site that checks for flight availability specifically under £99 or under £199. There is however, also the option for specific searches to be made for package holidays or flights only to a wide range of destinations.

Another feature is the up to date search facility which shows availability on discounted holidays which is updated every twenty minutes. In order to make the site easy to use, the homepage categorises the services and products available into three categories – Search & Buy which include This Weekend – a section with last minute deals on package holidays and flights. Other elements include Find a Holiday, Buy a Flight, Hire a Car, Travel Insurance and Winter Sports. The section titled

Planning, offers Destination Guides, a Resort Finder, Free Brochures, Live Weather, Prices by Email, Convert Money and a UK Airport Guide. With the final section, Our Service, a Help Desk is available, in addition to the Send a Postcard facility, which allows users to send email postcards with views from various holiday destinations. This section also features a Feedback Link and a facility for users to recommend the site to others.

## Promotion

Throughout 2000 Bargainholidays.com maximised its consumer reach through a combination of above and below-the-line techniques. While a great deal of PR was generated around its late availability deals, the Bargainholidays.com brand could be seen in a number of places. Taxi cabs, bus stops, on the sides of buildings, football and cricket boards were all covered with the Bargainholidays.com logo.

Throughout the year a great deal of press advertising was undertaken in national newspapers while a large scale cinema campaign ran during the summer months.

Online promotion through banner advertising and competitions also raised awareness of the Bargainholidays.com brand.

## Brand Values

Bargainholidays.com aims to be the best place to find discounted holidays online with the best deals combined with easy site navigation ensuring its accessibility to everyone.

## Future Plans

Bargainholidays.com has several planned routes for expanding its offering. These included the creation of an online booking service and a move towards the provision of Airport Services such as car parking and access to airport lounges. Another area which is being explored is the addition of cruises to the current range of holidays available.

**www.bargainholidays.com**

## Market Context

The internet has become a part of everyday life for many people over the last few years. There are over 23 million adults in the UK now accessing the internet (Source: ONS 2001).

An increasing number of people are using the internet for shopping – in the run up to Christmas 2000, UK shoppers spent £405 million through the internet (Source: British Retail Consortium). In addition, the introduction of interactive television services is set to bring the internet, and online shopping, into many more homes.

beeb.com is making the most of these trends – offering the online shopper advice and inspiration through its Shopping Guides along with the opportunity to shop safely and securely with beeb.com's trusted retailers partners.

## Achievements

Following the repositioning of the website as a trusted guide to online shopping and an extensive marketing campaign, beeb.com has become the fourth largest online shopping website in the UK (Source: MMXI November 2000), providing inspiration and advice through a range of BBC branded Shopping Guides.

This unique mix of editorial and e-commerce has helped beeb.com to top the table of online shopping portals in terms of maintaining consumer interest – the website has the highest ratio of web pages viewed per visitor (Source: MMXI 2001).

As well as making an impact on the internet, beeb.com has also led the way on interactive television, running services on NTL, Telewest, and ONdigital.

## Key Management

Since September 2000, Julian Turner has been Chief Executive Officer of beeb Ventures Ltd, the joint venture between BBC Worldwide and THLi, which manages beeb.com and BBC Worldwide's ISP beeb.net.

Julian joined from Granada Media, where he was Director of Online and Interactive Media – responsible for such brands as G-Wizz and working on

agreements with the likes of Ask Jeeves in partnership with Carlton. Julian's understanding of the internet business stems from the management positions he held at IBM (UK) Ltd, Oracle Corporation (UK) Ltd and Decision Systems International (Olivetti Group) prior to joining Granada Media.

Kym Niblock, Chief Operating Officer, beeb Ventures Ltd is responsible for the day to day management and technical aspects of running beeb.com and beeb.net.

Kym joined beeb Ventures Ltd in September 2000 from Nickelodeon International Limited, where she was Deputy Managing Director, VP. At Nickelodeon, Kym was most recently responsible for the management of business activities and operations of the company's European channels. Prior to that, Kym looked after Nickelodeon International's planning and launch activities as Director, Technical & Launch Operations.

Patrick Hannon, Chief Commercial Officer, beeb Ventures Ltd is responsible for business development, advertising sales, e-commerce partnerships and initiatives, as well as marketing and the brand awareness of beeb.com and beeb.net.

Patrick joined the company following three years as BBC Multimedia's Business Development Director, a role which saw him oversee the commercial development and international distribution of the BBC's range of interactive software. Prior to that he worked in the Corporate Strategy Unit, and in business development for EMAP Business Communications.

Drew Kaza has been Managing Director, Internet and Interactive for BBC Worldwide since September 1999. He is responsible for the management and development of a new combination of businesses within BBC Worldwide, which are linked by their common theme of New Media, Interactivity, Electronic Commerce and Customer Response. These include beeb Ventures Ltd, Audiocall, Broadcasting Data Services, Games/Multimedia and Galleon, interactive TV and international syndication.

Drew joined Worldwide after four years running his own international media company Mediaplex which focused on business development in the areas of broadcasting, digital and interactive media.

Prior to forming Mediaplex, Drew spent fifteen years in film, television and publishing. Most recently he was President of the

MGM/Paramount/Universal joint venture, United International Pictures Pay-TV Group. From 1983-1992 he worked in the cable communications industry in a variety of marketing and programming roles, both in the UK and originally in the US.

## Background

beeb.com is wholly owned by beeb Ventures Ltd, a subsidiary company of BBC Worldwide and THLi, Global Internet Managers, LP. It was previously developed in collaboration with ICL, the IT services company.

Launched as an entertainment portal in 1997, beeb.com has grown traffic, revenue and content rapidly, as the internet becomes a mainstream consumer medium. This growth, together with further commercial agreements with advertisers and portal websites has established beeb.com as a site guiding people's online purchases.

beeb.com features a number of Shopping Guides including Top Gear, Gardeners' World, Top of the Pops, Radio Times, Holiday and Good Homes. Additionally, it features webzines based on BBC Worldwide magazine brands such as Radio Times and allabouteve.co.uk.

## Product/Service

beeb.com is a guide to shopping online with trusted retailers. Through beeb.com's branded Shopping Guides and webzines, it provides direction and inspiration for online shoppers, whether they are experienced internet consumers looking for information and research, or new to the online environment.

The website provides a guide to buying a wide range of products across a diverse range of categories. If visitors to the site are looking for a dream holiday, books for the beach, a personal stereo for the long flight and music to listen to, beeb.com has provision for all these requirements. In addition, if visitors are looking to redecorate their house, redesign the garden, or even buy a new car, the site gives advice and guidance to buying the best products and services.

Through price value comparison technology, beeb.com gives visitors the chance to compare cost, delivery times and charges between retailers. This function compares the price of compact discs, videos, DVDs, books and even garden and house plants in seconds, helping consumers make the best choice on the internet.

## Promotion

Throughout Autumn 2000, beeb.com was promoted with a cross media

marketing campaign, that included television, radio and print advertising.

The campaign centred on a prime time TV advertisement with a creative theme aimed firmly at the mainstream audience, a markedly different strategy to many of the other dotcom campaigns. Evoking the classic Ladybird 'How it works' books of years gone by, the ads aimed to attract users with a clear and simple message aimed at both those who have yet to get online and those already experienced in online shopping.

The campaign was supported by a series of print adverts which appeared in national daily and Sunday papers as well as an extensive radio campaign. Additionally, a series of innovative promotions, offers and competitions were run. The Ladybird 'How it works' book, featured in the advertising was actually published, giving advice on how to shop on the internet and a beeb.com mobile internet café in a double decker bus went on a nationwide tour of shopping centres, offering shoppers the chance to experience how online shopping can be safe and easy, in a café environment.

## Brand Values

beeb.com provides a safe and secure online environment for consumers to shop.

It harnesses the power of popular BBC brands – such as Gardeners' World, Top of the Pops and Radio Times – to provide shopping inspiration and guides consumers to selected retail partners that meet strict security and customer care guidelines.

## Future Plans

beeb.com is positioned to take full advantage of future developments in internet shopping, and the development of interactive television services.

While the site itself will grow to include greater personalisation and options for users and an increasingly wide range of products, beeb.com's involvement in interactive television trials with BT Interactive (ADSL) and Microsoft Web TV as well as experience gained from providing services to NTL Telewest and ONdigital mean beeb.com is ideally placed to make the most of this emerging medium.

**www.beeb.com**

# blueyonder
hi-speed internet

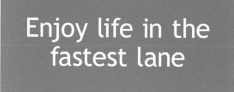

## Enjoy life in the fastest lane

Hi-speed Internet Access • Permanent Connection • Broadband Cable

Surf flat out on our new hi-speed blueyonder terminal

Telewest    blue yonder    www.blueyonder.co.uk/info

## Market Context

The internet has transformed the way we live, work and play. But it will be broadband technology which will bring online living to life and revolutionise the way people use the internet.

Broadband internet services open up a new online world for web users providing significantly improved access to online music, radio, video, news, sport, games and education.

Broadband cable internet access offers speeds nearly ten times faster than conventional dial-up services, making downloading web pages and information quicker and easier and the consumer's internet experience considerably richer.

Because a broadband internet connection is continuous and does not tie-up the telephone line, there are no more busy dial-up signals or frustrations over access to phone calls.

In March 2000 Telewest launched the UK's first consumer cable modem internet service, blueyonder hi-speed and the company is now at the forefront of the broadband revolution.

## Achievements

Telewest has continued to expand its portfolio of internet services which are now all marketed under the blueyonder ISP brand.

The range of blueyonder services fulfils the needs and expectations of all types of internet users, from experienced and savvy surfers to customers wanting to access the internet for the first time.

Telewest's blueyonder pay-as-you-go service offers reliable dial-up access for light users of the internet.

blueyonder surfunlimited, the first unlimited dial-up service in the UK, was launched on 14th February 2000, providing internet access for a fixed monthly fee with no call charges.

The blueyonder hi-speed service offers the ultimate internet experience with speeds nearly ten times faster than conventional dial-up access, a continuous broadband connection which doesn't tie-up the phone line and unlimited access for a fixed monthly fee.

At the end of 2000 Telewest had connected over 280,000 internet customers and its hi-speed service is the current broadband market share leader within the company's franchise areas.

Telewest sees internet provision as a key growth area and anticipates that the speed, reliability and customer focus of the blueyonder service will continue to attract strong consumer interest.

## Key Management

Gavin Patterson is Commercial Director for Internet and Telephony Services at Telewest, where he is responsible for the strategic development of products and day-to-day management of marketing and sales.

He led the launch of blueyonder hi-speed, the UK's first consumer broadband cable modem service, in March 2000.

Gavin joined Telewest in October 1999 and quickly developed his position into a combined marketing, product development and sales role. He is committed to providing a high level of network service to satisfy the customers' performance requirements.

The Cambridge University graduate was born in Altrincham, Cheshire and received a BA in Chemical Engineering in 1989, before returning to complete a Masters in Engineering in 1990. Gavin's career in the marketing industry began at Procter & Gamble.

Chad Raube is Head of Marketing for Internet Services at Telewest. He is responsible for the development and marketing of the blueyonder portfolio of residential internet services.

He also monitors the competitive and consumer landscape for new product development opportunities and key trends impacting the internet industry.

Before joining Telewest in June 2000, Chad worked in the internet industry in America, Asia and, most notably, in New Zealand, where he was General Manager of Cyberstar, a startup broadband service provider.

After matriculating from Harvard Business School, Chad was involved with the MediaOne Group and, in particular, with Road Runner hi-speed online – a joint venture between MediaOne, Time Warner, Compaq and Microsoft.

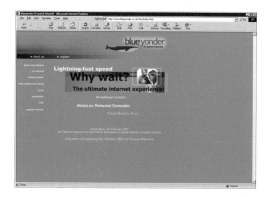

He has also worked on a consultative basis for senior executives at buyersaccess.com, a US-based B2B portal focused on the real estate industry.

## Background

blueyonder hi-speed was launched in March 2000, becoming the UK's first consumer cable modem internet service.

The service encapsulates Telewest's vision of revolutionising the internet through broadband technology and of providing a cutting edge internet access service at a competitive price.

## Product/Service

Telewest's advanced digital-ready network, combined with the group's content expertise, means it is uniquely positioned to provide for consumers' future broadband requirements.

At the end of 2000 blueyonder hi-speed was available to over four million homes across Telewest's UK franchises.

It offers access to the internet at nearly ten times the speed of a standard dial-up modem and brings the internet to life with richer content and instant downloads.

It is a continuous, 'always on' connection that doesn't tie up the phone line and enables you to use the internet quickly and conveniently, without the frustration of logging on and dialling up.

There are no phone call charges and blueyonder hi-speed offers value for money – a one-off installation fee of £50 and then £33 fixed fee per month – just over £1 a day for unlimited usage.

Users have 30MB of web space storage and five email accounts, each with three alias addresses, enabling family members to send and receive their own personal email.

Network performance is monitored regularly and customers are kept informed via email and newsgroups, and there is support too on other matters, including misuse of the ISP and security.

## Promotion

With the blueyounder hi-speed service available across all Telewest regions, marketing activity is being stepped up in 2001.

The promotional activity intends to bring to life the broadband world that blueyonder hi-speed offers consumers, through an integrated marketing campaign using both traditional and non-traditional creative and media.

The initial focus is on the 'seeing is believing' message. One challenge for 2001 has been to develop that idea further and take it to a wider audience. Media advertising has included inserts in national press, running concurrently with radio advertisements on major commercial stations. The key creative message is simple – 'why wait?' – which is built on insight gained from research, showing the frustration amongst

internet users with slow surfing.

Carefully targeted direct mail continues to be a vital acquisition tool, supported by online campaigns and banner advertising – raising the profile of blueyonder services to online consumers.

In addition, Telewest will use demonstration events and ambient, affiliate and loyalty programmes to complete an integrated marketing campaign aimed at bringing the benefits of the blueyonder services to life.

## Brand Values

blueyonder's vision is to use broadband technology to revolutionise the way consumers experience the internet. With blueyonder hi-speed the internet is fast, approachable and easy to use.

Living life in the blueyonder, however, is about much more than being the fastest, easiest way to be online.

It introduces consumers to an entirely new online world, full of excitement, exploration and learning opportunities, with improved access to music, information downloads, audio and video streaming, real time share dealing and 3D chat.

And, because the blueyonder hi-speed service provides a permanent connection, consumers have the freedom to use the internet when it suits them.

In a highly competitive market, it also represents best value in Telewest's franchise areas. blueyonder hi-speed's fixed monthly fee enables customers to explore the internet for as long as they want and experience the rich content and information that has made the world wide web the fastest growing technology in history.

## Future Plans

In the UK the scope and quality of digital services is unique. 'Convergence' will become an increasingly recurrent and familiar term for consumers.

To blueyonder customers in particular, internet content will become available across many household access devices – be they PC, TV or telephone (mobile and fixed line).

The internet will become an integral part of our lives, in the same way as the telephone and television, and broadband living will put users in real time interactive control of content across time, location and medium.

In addition, over the coming months and years, service providers like blueyonder will continue to add enhanced content and additional features, offering consumers personalised internet experiences.

It is all part of a vision in which blueyonder is leading the field – the reality of a fast, always on, broadband culture.

**www.blueyonder.co.uk**

# chello™

## Market Context

Broadband is one of the fastest growing and most dynamic sectors of the internet market. While dial-up ISPs continue to redefine themselves, the option of connecting to a high-speed, always-on service at a fixed monthly charge continues to prove increasingly attractive.

The appeal of broadband is particularly strong in Western Europe where estimates indicate that by 2004 more than a third of all internet connections will be broadband. This will mean a compound annual growth rate for broadband of 161% – resulting in a total of approximately 50 million subscribers.

This growth is fuelled by an appreciation by consumers that, while dial-up services may have been adequate in the early days of the web, they are increasingly limiting. Demand today and in the future will be for the interactivity and multimedia content which the internet has long promised but only broadband connections can deliver.

The big challenge for broadband ISPs is to manage the growth potential in both technological and content terms.

## Achievements

Against this backdrop of change, chello has grown to become the biggest broadband internet brand in Europe and the only broadband ISP which has a significant European multi-market presence.

Among chello's major achievements has been its dramatic growth – both in numbers of households subscribing to the service and countries in which it is available.

chello's latest subscriber figures – 340,000 at year end 2000 – represents a 220% growth in a year (from 106,500 in December 1999) and almost a ten-fold increase since the company's launch in

March 1999. It took chello less than nine months to break the 100,000 subscriber barrier – and just another eleven months to treble that figure.

In terms of market penetration, chello is active in ten countries: Australia, Austria, Belgium, Chile, France, Hungary, the Netherlands, Norway, Poland and Sweden.

Beyond market achievements, chello lays claim to some significant technological milestones, beginning with the creation of AORTA™ – Europe's first, fastest and largest broadband IP backbone network, delivering content at up to 2.5 Gbps. chello was also among the first to introduce advanced 'dense wave division multiplexing' technology to Europe.

chello has received numerous plaudits, including the Worldwide Ground Breaker Award for Marketing from Multichannel News International in 2000 and in June of that year TIME magazine named chello one of Europe's top 50 high-tech companies. In 1999 it was named Best Consumer ISP in Europe at the European ISP Awards.

## Key Management

Mitch Clarke, Executive Vice President of chello broadband access, has been with chello since its inception in 1998, as Vice President of Sales, and has been a member of the chello management board since 1999. Clarke joined chello from UPC Norway where he was Managing Director of UPC's first Scandinavian ISP.

Sudhir Ispahani, Chief Technical Officer of chello and Chairman of the UPC Technology Board, is the technology visionary behind chello, responsible for designing, implementing and supporting all aspects of technology and systems deployment. Previously, Ispahani was Director of Service Direct at MCI in the US.

Rob Shepherd, Executive Vice President of chello interactive services, oversees all portal operations and UPC interactive TV operations, UPCtvi. Shepherd's career encompasses fifteen years in general and technology management roles.

Paul Bridge, Vice President Marketing, has overall responsibility for marketing. Before joining chello he was Senior Vice President of Marketing and Sales at Bank One International, and was previously Vice President of Acquisition Marketing at American Express Europe Ltd.

## Background

In November 1998, chello's parent company, United Pan-Europe Communications, fired up its broadband backbone AORTA™ service. Three months later, chello went live in five countries across Europe – the Netherlands, Norway, Belgium, France and Austria.

Since that time, chello has become Europe's biggest broadband brand, increased its reach into central Europe and pioneering high-speed internet via satellite as well as cable.

## Product/Service

chello offers high-speed, next-generation internet access. It delivers significantly faster access than traditional dial-up modems (even with ISDN), alongside other associated cable broadband benefits such as constant connection, fixed monthly fee, and no associated telephone charges. This means that downloading software becomes fast and easy, entertainment becomes more compelling and up-to-the-minute information is available on demand.

In each market, the chello brand presents an easy-to-use local-language portal, featuring carefully-selected broadband content including a full range of top-quality channels covering news, entertainment, communications and interactive games, tailored to local, national and international consumers.

## Promotion

Integrated marketing campaigns are core to the establishment of chello as Europe's leading broadband company. chello recognises the need to educate and familiarise consumers with new technology and uses advertising, promotions, demonstrations and PR to convey the message and provide opportunities for consumers to experience the chello service firsthand.

The 'hello, I'm chello' advertising campaign concept aims at introducing the brand to the consumer and its technology to the early adopters in each market. Executing the campaign through-the-line has seen chello take the technology to the consumer using promotions in high profile public areas such as international airports as well as in the heart of the communities – using demo vehicles such as 'the broadband bus' and 'transport icons' such as trams and buses.

## Brand Values

chello has rapidly established a distinctive brand personality that sets it apart from its competitors. The 'hello I'm chello' campaign has created a fun, friendly and accessible personality. This has been rigorously applied across multiple markets. The chello brand vision is all about making people's lives easier, fuller, happier and richer, in short a more colourful life. Also the sponsorship of the Arrows Formula One team, has given the brand a positive association of speed and technology, and has contributed substantially to the increase in awareness across global markets.

## Future Plans

Building on the success of Europe's fastest and largest broadband backbone, forthcoming activity is focused on the launch of chello broadband's interactive TV service – chello TV provides the customer with a full range of interactive services that can be accessed via the television set. Using the TV remote control, customers can get up-to-the-minute local and national news, weather and entertainment information as well as being able to play games, shop and send emails.

**www.chello.com**

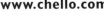

**web application server**

## Market Context

We are now in the next phase of the ebusiness revolution. It is about having more than a website. It is about being e-enabled. It is about delivering a truly memorable web experience to the consumer.

Businesses and consumers are fuelling this next phase in the new economy. Customers require ever more sophisticated websites, delivering greater levels of functionality and richer end-user experiences. It is marketeers that are ultimately responsible for making sure this happens.

By definition, you only ever get one chance to make a first impression. Living up to customer expectations is a prerequisite for building loyalty. A company's website is often the first critical 'window' to the rest of the organisation.

Businesses now have to e-enable their operations. To succeed, suppliers and customer organisations need to do the same. Rosabeth Moss Kanter, The Harvard Business School guru, recently highlighted the issues businesses are facing commenting that "ebusiness leaders need to embrace radical rather than cosmetic organisation change – painting lipstick on a bulldog doesn't make it any more beautiful."

It is within this dynamic, fast moving environment that Macromedia's ColdFusion is helping businesses to deliver dynamic sites that drive their business. It is not just about developing a site. This is just the start. It is about enabling companies, their suppliers and their customers.

Getting this right means companies can save money and increase levels of service across the value chain from e-procurement to just-in-time processes.

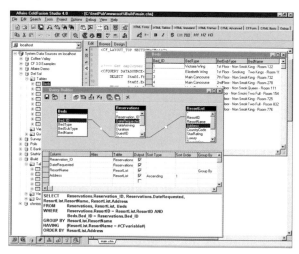

## Achievements

How ColdFusion is perceived externally is crucial. The product has received numerous industry awards including, in March 2001, the Software and Information Industry Association's (SIIA) prestigious Codie Award for Best Application development product.

ColdFusion is used by over half of the Fortune 500 companies to create websites across a range of industries from insurance to publishing.

## Key Management

Jeremy Allaire, Chief Technology Officer, Macromedia, helps to drive the company's future product direction. Jeremy is Macromedia's primary technology evangelist and has directed the development of Allaire's award winning products. He led Allaire's emergence into the packaged applications marketplace with the development and heralded the introduction of Allaire Spectra.

Simon Frank, Regional Manager of Northern Europe, has over twenty years experience in the IT industry, Simon joined Allaire in April 1999. As one of the first European employees, Simon helped to build the Allaire infrastructure and drive sales of ColdFusion, as well as Spectra and Java products; JRun and Kawa in the UK, Scandinavia and Africa. Simon is also a Best Practice evangelist.

Ben Forta, ColdFusion evangelist, has over fifteen years of experience as a software developer, and has been involved in several commercial applications including the launch of two successful internet-based companies. Forta co-authored the official Allaire ColdFusion training courses, and provides on-site ColdFusion training and consulting for corporations. Additionally, he has written best sellers on ColdFusion, HomeSite and SQL.

## Background

ColdFusion is now one of the flagship products of Macromedia Inc. On March 20 2001 Macromedia and Allaire merged and now operate under the Macromedia name. Macromedia is headquartered in San Francisco, California, US with offices throughout the world.

The overall corporate aim of the merged company is to enable web professionals to efficiently develop web content and applications on multiple devices. Macromedia now services over two million web professionals.

Allaire brothers JJ and Jeremy founded Allaire early in 1995 when they launched ColdFusion. ColdFusion, a popular web development tool, drives tens of thousands of enterprise and e-commerce applications in leading companies worldwide. Some of its customers include Siemens, The European Commission, Boeing, 192.com and Freeserve.

ColdFusion's focus is on the mass enterprise market, which includes

Global 2000 corporations, local and national government and large educational institutions. This is the prime target because the mass enterprise is where ColdFusion really shines because it is fast to implement, accessible, highly productive, scalable and can be applied to a wide range of requirements across multiple platforms.

## Product/Service

ColdFusion is the cornerstone of the Macromedia platform. It provides both the development tools and runtime platform required for developing and delivering applications on the web.

It is one of the most widely adopted cross-platform commercial web application servers on the market, running Windows NT, Sun Solaris, HP-UX, and Linux.

ColdFusion makes it easier for the less sophisticated web developer to get a dynamic site up and running in a short time. Yet it is powerful enough to be at the core of large, complex commerce sites.

A key benefit of ColdFusion is scalability. All sizes of companies from the very largest multinational corporation, receiving millions of hits a day, to small start-up companies can use it.

## Promotion

The integrated B2B marketing campaign focuses mainly on below-the-line activity. PR is one of the most effective methods of reaching a targeted audience of web developers. The global PR campaign focuses on raising ColdFusion's profile in the key trade press. Activities such as securing covermounts and reviews of the latest versions of the software are important to keep the product front of mind for developers.

Third party endorsement in the leading trade press is essential for ColdFusion's profile. Some recent comments have come from PC Magazine who said "ColdFusion is built for the web and is a tried-and-true solution on large commercial sites such as Autobytel.com, showing its scalability. The development environment is powerful, and the product has extensive third-party and ISP support. Developers will find this a firm foundation for web applications."

New Media Magazine commented "ColdFusion is ideal for building data-heavy sites with dynamically generated pages – everything from a fantasy sports league to an e-commerce site."

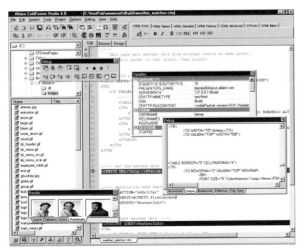

The views of the analyst community are equally important. Recent comments from major analyst groups have included Butler Group stating "Companies require Web Application Servers that will provide scalability, high availability and robustness. Allaire

Corporation (recently merged with Macromedia) has developed an Application Server, ColdFusion, which supplies all of these benefits. It is the foundation and building block to the company's range of ebusiness products."

Regular user conferences cement relationships and maintain dialogue with web developers. An executive seminar series sponsored by Deloitte & Touche, Sprint E-Solutions and Fig Leaf has also been launched in the US.

Channel partnerships are central to Macromedia's communication strategy. The merged company has a network of over 2000 partners (with over 105 in the UK) delivering integrated web application development and business solutions to customers across the world.

The merged company also has strategic partners including Microsoft, Compaq, CSC, Deloitte & Touche and IBM.

Macromedia attends trade shows throughout Europe – including Internet World held on 5-7 June 2001 in London.

## Brand Values

The ColdFusion web application server aims to give a fastest way to develop and deliver scalable enterprise and e-commerce business applications. It can revolutionise a company's HR operations, build the next generation of your firm's global intranet or even launch the next successful dotcom company.

## Future Plans

ColdFusion remains a key product in the new company's portfolio. ColdFusion 5.0 was launched on April 30 2001 and demonstrates the value of the merged Allaire and Macromedia. Neo will make the power of CFMl available on J2EE. The vision for ColdFusion is to become the mindshare and marketshare leader among aspiring web application developers who place a premium on empowerment, rapid development and ease of use. IDC, the market research company forecasts strong continued growth in the application server market. The market is expected to exceed US$5 billion in 2001 and US$11 billion in 2004.

The merger has also been welcomed in the industry. Forrester Europe research group said "the combined company will offer a strong development platform".

**www.macromedia.com**

# deal4free.com™

## Market Context

Back in the late 1980s and early 1990s the financial markets seemed a daunting place for the ordinary investor. Steeped in mystique and somewhat inaccessible, the City gave the impression that financial markets were an exclusive club that the general public was excluded from joining. Everyone can recall images of the stripy and colourful jackets of the yuppie futures traders, the pin-stripe suit and braces of the trusted stockbroker, and the grey suit of the stony-faced bank manager. However two major events changed the attitudes of both the financial industry and the ordinary investor. Firstly, ordinary people started owning shares when the government privatised national industries. Secondly, the widespread adoption of the internet by the public.

The internet has given the ordinary investor the power to make the financial industry stand up and listen as smaller and more agile companies have emerged that allow customers to become trader, broker and banker. The information and decision making material used by the financial industry in the past can now be passed down to the ordinary investor electronically at a fraction of the cost.

It is generally accepted that the internet has profoundly affected financial markets, perhaps more so than any other sector of commerce. UK online share trading accounts are expected to rise from 200,000 in 2000 to 1.8 million by 2004.

## Achievements

In 1996 CMC Group plc (CMC), owner of the deal4free.com brand, was the first company in the world to offer real time foreign exchange (FX) dealing over the internet. Within a matter of months, customers using the new online trading software were trading $1 billion a month. Since 1996 the product has gone from strength to strength. In 1998 the software used by deal4free.com received the coveted Millennium Product Award from the UK Government for outstanding technical innovation in the 1990s.

Since inception deal4free.com has traded over $150 billion online and has carried out over one million deals.

deal4free.com became one of the first companies in the world to trade the new European currency by executing two million Euros at 10pm on Sunday 3rd January 1999 over the internet.

deal4free.com has also been recognised as the top privately owned e-commerce company in Europe by the Sunday Times e-league. deal4free.com scored a near perfect 26 points out of a possible 27 for technology.

With customers in over 55 countries around the world, these achievements have made deal4free.com the leading global brand for online margin trading. An impressive 30% of customers who sign up with deal4free.com join because of third party recommendation.

## Key Management

Peter Cruddas, Managing Director and Founder, has over 25 years experience in the City of London having advised government agencies and banking institutions on how to set up their own dealing operations. Peter is the chief strategist and the inspiration behind the deal4free brand. He was the creator of the deal4free.com brand name and is involved in the marketing of the brand on a day-to-day basis.

Roger Hynes, Chief Operating Officer, started his career in corporate finance and advertising before joining deal4free.com as Marketing Director. Roger is now Chief Operating Officer of the CMC Group and is involved in all the marketing communications behind the deal4free brand, as well as general management of the company.

## Background

deal4free.com was the brainchild of Peter Cruddas. His inspiration for the brand was formed in 1994 when he saw the potential benefits of integrating financial services and the internet. He realised very early that the internet was the perfect tool to offer a significant number of smaller investors the ultimate trading service, but at a fraction of the traditional cost. Previously telephone based trading had only allowed one dealer to quote one customer at any one time. The internet now permits one dealer to instantly quote to 10,000 customers in real-time, allowing a substantial enhancement of trading speed and cost efficiency. Instead of increasing the profit margin Peter chose to pass the large cost savings down to the customer. Thus the concept of free trading was born. deal4free.com decided

to give free to the customer a number of investor information services such as real time news feeds, charting and market analysis. These free services would potentially equate to thousands of pounds worth of savings for deal4free.com trading customers.

As the business expanded the product and service received more and more press recognition, allowing the company to remain highly profitable and self-financing. As the traditional image of trading in the City finally began to be dismantled piece by piece, the balance of power started to shift towards the ordinary investor. deal4free had been instrumental in kick-starting the customer revolution.

releases were used to generate further interest in the brand by informing the media about how deal4free had become the first trading company to offer customer commission free trading. As interest in deal4free grew it was discussed on Bloomberg TV and The Money Channel.

Online advertising consisted of banners, keyword purchasing, search engine optimisation, direct e-mails and strategic sponsorship. Banners and sponsorship appeared on major online financial information sites including Interactive Investors, Hemscott.net and Sharepages.com. Attendance at online trading exhibitions promoted brand awareness and cemented consumer trust.

## Product/Service

Unlike many other dotcom businesses, deal4free.com has not sought to 'cut and paste' an old business model onto the internet. deal4free.com employs twice as many software programmers than dealers in order to ensure that the deal4free.com software is at the forefront of online trading technology. The deal4free.com service allows customers to trade UK, US, and European shares and Indices as Contract for Differences (CFD). Other products include foreign exchange, currency options, and precious metals all from a single account 24-hours a day. At the touch of a button customers have access to trade in over 2000 instruments. A customer can be in Australia trading a UK stock during US trading hours all within seconds and totally free of commission. deal4free.com has helped increase customers expectations in terms of price, speed and quality of service. Very few online trading company's presently offer deal4free.com's unique fusion of cutting edge trading software, comprehensive product range and cost saving opportunities.

## Promotion

A combination of online and offline advertising as well as PR raised brand awareness. Advertising strategy was based around deal4free's unique selling proposition of commission free trading. Adverts were designed to create intrigue and curiosity. Using the website as an educational and promotional tool, all traditional press and electronic banner adverts were designed to drive potential customers to the deal4free.com website. The website was built around the fact that customers could trial the trading software with no financial risk.

To begin with deal4free used extensive offline advertising in all major financial publications including The Financial Times, The Times, The Sunday Business and Investors Chronicle. In addition, strategic London Underground stations were chosen to run the same messages. Press

## Brand Values

The brand philosophy at CMC sits comfortably with its business philosophy of being able to offer customers commission free dealing via the internet. The deal4free.com brand embodies seven years of dedicated hard work in bringing the highest quality software to the online trading market. Since its inception deal4free.com has gained integrity because it offers a service to those people who wished to trade but were previously denied access to markets.

The aim behind deal4free.com was to create a brand that instantly describes the product, explains the proposition, allows instant access to information and defines how the product will be distributed.

It is important that when people see the deal4free brand they quickly come to recognise what is being offered – commission free trading in thousands of instruments on award winning software, with free information contained within an online trading platform that is accessible from anywhere in the world.

## Future Plans

2001 witnesses a number of important product, software and service enhancements. There will be the release of a web based Java version of the trading software, the introduction of many more new global instruments and the extension of the traditional market hours to 'out of hours' trading, eventually leading to a 24-hour trading day.

deal4free.com will also be introducing a new spread-betting service in 2001, which will allow clients to bet on the price movement of a comprehensive range of financial products traded in the City.

deal4free.com will also be looking to expand into mainland Europe and Asia by the end of 2001 in order to reinforce the brands global appeal.

**www.deal4free.com**

# eBay.co.uk

## Market Context

Given the popularity of car boot sales it is no surprise that the online auction market has taken off dramatically over the past five years. Not that the quality of items you would find on an online auction site would bear much resemblance to the wares on offer at most car boot sales, but as forums for trading an eclectic mix of goods they have much in common. The online auction market has captured people's imagination because it really harnesses the potential of the internet at a local and global level as a trading medium which has no offline equivalent.

The UK online auction market consists of four key players: eBay, QXL, FSAuctions and Yahoo! Auctions.

eBay pioneered online auctions when it was founded in the US in 1995, with the UK site launching four years later. In a short space of time, eBay.co.uk has grown to become the leading online person-to-person trading community in the UK.

## Achievements

eBay is a truly global company enabling users worldwide to trade items on a national and international level. With over 22.5 million registered users (as at March 2001) worldwide, approximately 60 regional sites in the US and nine country-specific sites globally, eBay has become one of the greatest ecommerce success stories today.

Since its launch in the UK in October 1999, eBay.co.uk has become the largest person-to-person trading community in the country and, once online, people stay there with eBay UK being one of the 'stickiest' sites in the UK.

eBay has received a raft of awards and distinctions, for instance, in 2000, it was judged Entrepreneurial Company of the Year by the Harvard Business School and was also voted as one of Vanity Fair's top 50 E-Establishments and won the MIT Sloan School of Business' Global Reach Award.

As well as being the UK's premier online trading site, eBay.co.uk has proved to be an innovative way for UK charities to boost their income. With access to eBay's 22.5 million-plus registered users around the world, the eBay network of sites afford huge fund-raising potential to charities.

CHhugs (Children's Hospice Hugs), for instance, has seen its funds treble since it started auctioning off celebrity-signed beanie-babies online at eBay. Other charities which have benefited from auctions on eBay include the Whale and Dolphin Conservation Society, Breakthrough Breast Cancer and the NSPCC.

## Key Management

Pierre Omidyar, Chairman and Founder, was an early internet enthusiast, and worked in some of the most visionary companies in Silicon Valley before founding eBay in 1995. He worked for Apple subsidiary Claris and for other Mac-oriented software development companies before co-founding Ink Development Corporation in 1991, taking it into the uncharted waters of internet shopping two years later. By the time it was sold to Microsoft in 1996, Omidyar was working for General Magic, where he developed the first web application for Magic Cap and contributed to other significant internet projects.

Chief Executive Officer, Meg Whitman was previously General Manager of Hasbro's Pre-School division, responsible for Global Management and Marketing of two of the world's best known children's brands, Playskool and Mr Potato Head. Meg oversaw the reorganisation and return to profitability of the division. Prior to this she was President and CEO of Florists Transworld Delivery, the world's largest floral products company. Her earlier career included spells with the Walt Disney Company, Bain & Co and Procter & Gamble.

Michael van Swaaij, Vice President, Europe is responsible for bringing eBay's unique online person-to-person trading community to all the major European internet markets. eBay's vision is to allow Europe's buyers and sellers to trade within their own countries, across Europe and around the world. Before joining eBay he held senior positions at AOL Bertelsmann Online, which he helped set up and flourish in Europe. As Regional Managing Director and member of the AOL-Europe

executive team, he was responsible for the CompuServe service in the UK, as well as the AOL and CompuServe operations and activities in Scandinavia, Benelux and southern Europe.

Jennifer Mowat, Country Manager, eBay UK aims to continue the ascent of eBay within the UK market, developing the site to meet local interests and the individual needs of traders in the UK. Jennifer was formerly Head of Marketing at Associated New Media, one of the UK's largest commercial online publishers, where she helped build some of the industry's best known brands, including the award-winning ThisisLondon.co.uk. Before that she was Marketing Communications Manager at Agency.com, one of Europe's largest web development houses, with clients including RSPCA, Boots the Chemist and General Motors.

and interest-specific discussion forums where users gather daily to discuss everything from the latest addition to their collection to what the weather's like in their area.

Many eBay users have created a second business, or ditched their day jobs completely, by selling items on eBay. For others, eBay is the place to share a passion for items that are special to them. The sense of community is alive and well offline too. It has been known for eBay users go on holiday together, group together to buy some high value items and even get together to do home repairs for others.

## Background

A casual dinner conversation between Pierre Omidyar and his wife changed the face of internet commerce and sparked the development of one of the strongest online communities in the world. Mrs Omidyar, an avid Pez collector (Pez are colourful sweets dispensers), expressed a desire to be able to collect Pez dispensers and interact with other collectors over the internet. Pierre saw the potential of a central location where people could buy and sell unique items and meet users with similar interests and he launched eBay in September 1995.

**sports** football memorabilia — Buy / Sell

**sports** — Buy / Sell

**sports** going, going, gone-on-line. — Buy / Sell

**sports** You can buy and sell anything on eBay. eBay.co.uk

The key to eBay's success is trust and eBay goes to great lengths to create a safe trading environment. For example, eBay's Feedback Forum enables eBay users to leave comments about each other's buying and selling experiences. If you're a bidder, you can check your seller's Feedback Profile before you place a bid to learn about the other person's reputation with previous buyers. If you're a seller, do the same with your bidders.

## Product/Service

eBay is the world's largest personal online trading community. Individuals use eBay to buy and sell items in auctions across thousands of diverse categories, from china to computers, teddy bears to trains and furniture to figurines. At any one time there are five million auctions live on the site, and 650,000 new items are added every day.

eBay enables trade on a local, national or international basis, with 60 markets in the US alone as well as country sites in the Australia, Canada, France, Germany, Italy, Japan, Korea and the UK.

But the eBay community uses the site for more than trade. Users typically exchange emails during any trade and many friendships have been formed on the back of shared interests. eBay encourages this interaction and helps facilitate the sense of community by providing general

It does not happen often, but should there be a misuse of the system, eBay's SafeHarbour programme springs into action endeavouring to resolve issues in many areas such as fraud, trading offences, and illegally listed items.

## Promotion

eBay's marketing and promotional strategy focuses on promoting the eBay name to the niche communities who have a real connection with what trading on eBay could offer them – from collectors of antiques, toys and sports memorabilia to small businesses needing to buy one-off office supplies which could include anything from modems to office chairs to computer monitors. Principally focused online, marketing campaigns are highly targeted rather than via mass market advertising channels.

## Brand Values

eBay aims to enable people to buy or sell practically anything online. The eBay brand personality is fun, optimistic, down to earth, intriguing, empathetic and friendly. It is a family, community orientated brand.

## Future Plans

eBay aims to be the premier online trading site in the UK and to continue to develop and refine the service for the benefit of its users.

**www.ebay.co.uk**

## Market Context

Researching and booking discount travel is one of the leading sectors in the £2 billion UK e-commerce market. Currently, the online leisure travel market generates around £600 million in UK sales and rapid growth is expected to push this figure to £3.7 billion by 2005. This will account for 14% of all travel sales (Source: Forrester).

According to PhoCusWright, an internet travel intelligence company, ebookers.com is Europe's leading online travel agency, with sales of around £100 million per year. This gives ebookers a commanding 20% share of the online travel agency market, putting it well ahead of rivals such as Thomas Cook (6%).

Agencies like ebookers compete in the online travel market against suppliers such as airlines like easyJet and Ryanair. PhoCusWright estimates that suppliers' websites account for 74% of the online travel market, with agencies accounting for the remaining 26%. However, ebookers and other agencies are expected to increase their share as the agency model offers a more comprehensive range of services to the consumer than suppliers can provide. Consequently, PhoCusWright says agencies' share will increase to 29% in 2002.

## Achievements

ebookers is now Europe's biggest online travel agency, with a 20% market share. This premier status is reflected in other notable accolades, such as being ranked the UK's leading travel website in the highly regarded Nielsen//NetRatings. In July 2000 Nielsen//NetRatings calculated that ebookers had a unique audience of 250,000 – 25% higher than its nearest competitor. This success has continued, and, at the end of 2000, ebookers had 740,000 registered users.

Unlike many other B2C brands in the unstable dotcom world, ebookers has enjoyed relatively strong commercial success. In July 2000 it successfully raised secondary funding of US$45 million, making it the only European B2C internet company to achieve this since the previous March. For the fourth quarter of 2000, ebookers announced a four-fold leap in gross sales

to £30 million. Buoyed by these results, the company began trading on the London Stock Exchange's Tech Mark on April 23 2001, adding to its position on the technology-rich Neuer Market and Nasdaq indices.

## Key Management

Dinesh Dhamija is the Founding Chief Executive of ebookers.com. He founded Flightbookers, the London-based travel company, in 1983. He has more than twenty years experience in the travel industry and was an internet pioneer when he established the UK's first interactive travel website for Flightbookers in 1996. Dinesh also gained crucial experience in the travel sector as European Regional Director for Royal Nepal Airlines.

ebookers' Managing Director is Dr Sanjiv Talwar. Prior to joining ebookers, he was Chairman of Talwar and Company, a chartered accounting, tax and investment company, which he founded in 1991. Sanjiv has also served as a senior professional on the European Corporate Investment Team of Investcorp International Ltd. He has also worked as a consultant for KPMG Peat Marwick and Coopers and Lybrand (now PricewaterhouseCoopers).

Chief Marketing Officer, Glenn Trouse, joined ebookers from the leading UK advertising agency, Grey Europe, where he served as Director of Emerging Markets. His long career in advertising has also seen him work for McCann Erickson and Bates Worldwide.

## Background

ebookers evolved as a spin-off from Flightbookers, the London-based travel company founded by Dinesh Dhamija in 1983. It was later established as a separate company, in June 1999, and in September of the same year, its new and enhanced user-friendly website was launched.

In November 1999, ebookers floated on the Nasdaq and Neuer Market, providing the company with funds to fuel its rapid European expansion.

In March 2000, ebookers became the first online travel agency to expand into ten European countries when it acquired travel agencies in Denmark and the Netherlands. When it launched its service in France and Finland, ebookers was the first interactive travel website.

In October 2000, ebookers acquired Flightbookers in a US$15 million deal. The acquisition is important because Flightbookers provides UK ticket fulfilment for ebookers. The deal means that in the UK, like each one of its eleven European markets, ebookers now has its own ticket fulfilment capability. This has become an important differentiator for the brand, as it allows ebookers to deal directly with customers rather than via a third party. It also boosts profitability by allowing it to retain the margins on fulfilment operations and to benefit from further cost efficiencies and economies of scale.

The deal also gave ebookers access to Flightbookers' 220,000 customers and to more discount negotiated fare relationships with airlines and travel licences. Flightbookers has long established negotiated arrangements with 56 airlines, offering customers discounts of up to 65% on published prices.

## Product/Service

ebookers stands out from its competitors by selling the full range of airfares – published fares, negotiated fares and 'distressed' last minute inventory. It has negotiated fare arrangements with 120 airlines and 14,000 hotels.

ebookers has offices in eleven countries: Denmark, Finland, France, Germany, Ireland, Netherlands, Norway, Spain, Sweden, Switzerland, with its head office in the UK. These territories account for 86% of Europe's online population. A key part of this Europe-wide service is to tailor each country's website to serve the local language and consumer preferences. The sites are served by local call centres to aid customers who are unaccustomed to internet bookings.

As well as offering competitive airfares, ebookers also offers car hire, hotel booking, travel insurance, package holidays and goods through an online travel shop.

The site attracts over two million visits per month and ebookers has nearly one million registered users. As well as the main travel site, ebookers has expanded its offering, launching a flight auctions service in January 2001 and a financial services arm, ebookersfinance.com, in September 2000. It has also entered the European ski market by launching ebookers.com ski micro sites in all of its European markets. The product covers a selection of 230 European resorts.

In November 2000, ebookers signed agreements with three major cruise lines – Star Cruises, Cunard and Carnival – to sell cruise holiday packages with secured negotiated discounts.

As well as these core product areas, ebookers offers other branded services to improve the customer experience and attract more business. These include Flight Watch – a flight status information service sent to mobile phone users via SMS. It also offers Fare Alert – an email notification

service alerting customers of attractive deals. For the flight auction service, ebookers has developed Bid and Go – a system where customers indicate the maximum they are willing to pay for a ticket and receive a reply within 24 hours.

## Promotion

ebookers is a prominent advertiser in the dotcom community but has not spent as much on high profile media as some of its competitors. Some of its more noticable campaigns include ads on London buses and the London Underground and ten second commercials on Virgin Radio.

More important to ebookers are strategic agreements with key interactive media owners. For example, June 2000, it signed a deal with NTL, the UK digital cable TV company. This sees ebookers providing content for NTL's interactive TV services, allowing consumers to buy from ebookers via their TV sets. This ebookers.com digital TV service appears on NTL's Travel Channel and provides an important promotional platform for the brand, reaching consumers who couldn't previously be reached because they didn't have a PC.

ebookers has established other valuable marketing partnerships, such as an agreement to be the exclusive flight service provider for AOL Europe. This means ebooker.com's flight-booking services are 'live' on all of AOL Europe's online services and web-based brands in the France, Germany and UK. The extra revenues from AOL – an extremely powerful ally – are proving a significant boost to ebookers' business.

Other important alliances include a deal with France Telecom which provides mobile telephone customers with access to ebookers' travel search engine. It has also signed partnership deals with Egg, Carphone Warehouse and Chelsea Football Club to provide exclusive travel services via interactive portals.

## Brand Values

ebookers.com is a complete one-stop-shop, offering a full range of travel products and services. The brand is about getting the best possible value for the customer, giving them the confidence that they could not find a better deal elsewhere.

## Future Plans

Looking to the future, ebookers will aim to continue to be one of Europe's strongest and largest online travel agencies.

**www.ebookers.com**

# egg: | Individual Money Matters

## Market Context

The high street banks have dominated the UK retail financial services market for many years and were very content to let this situation continue.

Financial services is a low interest area for most consumers and their inertia has been a continuous feature of Britain's attitude to finance – at least this was the situation until the creation of the online brand Egg.

When Egg launched in 1998, the only competition came from the high street banks. Two years on, the competitive environment is very different with other online entrants as well as many established offline banks launching their own separate internet brands, using equally unconventional sounding names such as Cahoot and IF.

Now 34% of all internet users visit a bank website and 21% had visited a financial service website in the last four weeks. The use of the Internet has become established as a major channel for customers. Egg has an 8% share of online savings accounts and 27% share of online credit cards (Source: internet User Profile Wave 11). Key groups opting to bank online are those people aged 25 to 44 and in high-income brackets.

## Achievements

Egg proved to be extremely successful during its launch phase in 1998. It exploited its first-mover advantage and is the one that all the others seek to beat. In the short time since its launch, Egg has achieved an overall brand consideration that places it 11th out of all financial services companies beating the likes of many long established brands in the industry (Source: Mori Future Buyer Behaviour Dec 2000).

Egg has 1.575 million customers (as at March 31 2001), which is roughly six times more than its nearest standalone competitor. With an 88% brand awareness score (Source: Hall & Partners), Egg is only slightly behind the more established brands such as Barclays and Halifax – a remarkable feat given that Egg is only two years old. Egg.com is now the 3rd most visited e-commerce site in Europe (Source: Jupiter MMXI Europe).

Egg also won the CIM/ Marketing Week Marketing Effectiveness Grand Prix in 1999 as well as winner of the Marketing Week Marketing Effectiveness Financial Services Brand of the year in 2000.

## Key Management

Paul Gratton, Chief Executive Officer, worked at First Direct in a variety of positions, including Financial Services Director, from 1989. Paul then joined Prudential Banking plc in 1996 as Operations Director, becoming Chief Operating Officer and then Deputy Chief Executive of Egg from its launch in October 1998. In January 2001, he became Chief Executive Officer of Egg.

Tony Williams, Director of Brand & Communications, started his career with TSB and was heavily involved in its transition from a savings organisation to a fully-fledged bank. He joined First Direct in 1989, with the firm belief that customers were no longer prepared to accept the levels of service offered by the traditional banks. In 1995, he joined the RAC with the objective of refreshing a traditional brand, while simultaneously arresting the declining membership. In 1998, Tony joined the project team to launch Egg, the UK's first bespoke internet bank.

## Background

Egg was launched by Prudential in October 1998 after several months of development and research. It was the UK's first ever internet bank and has been at the forefront of the digital revolution. Building a strong consumer brand in a highly commoditised product-led market, generating continuous awareness without a high street presence and creating a credible brand image amongst a highly cynical audience was no mean feat.

At launch an internal assessment by Egg, based upon research carried out by the Henley Centre - found that in fifteen years time, two in every three products, which are sold in the financial services will be sold via e-commerce. In today's money, that is over £200 billion a year. There is considerable evidence that this change is well underway, in 2000 alone, 16% of internet users had purchased financial services products remotely (Source: NOP Internet Tracking).

A survey indicates that nearly 23 million people in the UK were online by mid 2001 and fourteen million people will expect to use a new technology product for the first time. By 2006, it is expected that fourteen million people will be depending on new technology for banking, ten million for shopping and six million for investments (Source: MORI).

E-commerce gave Egg the opportunity to create a new generation of financial service company, built from scratch around customers' needs. Its initial challenge was to create a new brand that stood out in the market and really met the needs of consumers. The ongoing challenge it now faces is to ensure that the brand stays at the forefront of e-commerce by continuing to innovate in terms of products, customer service and communication.

Egg plc floated on June 12 2000, raising proceeds of approximately £150 million and is listed on the London Stock Exchange. Prudential plc continues to hold 79% of the share capital.

## Product/Service

Egg is tailor made for each individual customer, offering a range of savings, mortgage and insurance and investment products as well as an internet credit card.

Egg launched with a straightforward and a simple offer – all savings, from-as little as £1, will earn a top rate of interest in the Egg Savings Account. The popularity of this offer was unprecedented and new depositors overwhelmed the organisation proving that Egg's insight had been right and that the demand for competitive products, especially when backed up by a new and interesting brand, was huge.

A year later in October 1999, Egg Card was launched. The first true credit card designed for the internet, Egg Card offered customers hassle-free servicing on the internet as well as a market-leading offer and a cashback deal. Compared with the market leaders such as Barclaycard, Egg offered its customers a deal that was unheard of, putting considerable pressure on the competition. It now commands a 9% market share of all credit cards sold in the UK (Source: MORI MFS tracking survey).

Egg has also diversified into intermediation. Instead of always manufacturing own-label products, Egg has opted to distribute other brands products to customers via the internet. This means that customers can get the benefit of top quality products at a fraction of the usual cost. Egg Invest has created a Fund Supermarket where customers can choose from a wide range of unit trusts and ISAs from several fund managers.

Egg Insure also offers motor, home, life and travel insurance through a panel of insurers where the customer can benefit from the most competitive quote and choose which cover best suits their circumstances.

Egg Shop was also created to increase traffic to the website and consumers can transact with a number of online retailers where their purchases are guaranteed against online fraud by Egg.

## Promotion

Egg has used TV advertising extensively since launch, as it has proved essential in building a strong customer base. The Zoë Ball and Linford Christie launch ads promoted the Egg Savings Account and reflected Egg's attitude as well as aiming to challenge the conventions of financial services advertising by subverting its traditional use of celebrity endorsement.

At the core of its communication is the brand message - Egg: individual money matters.

It wanted commercials which embodied Egg brand values and established its tone of voice whilst normalising Egg as a brand name, backed up with a strong and motivating offer.

Similarly, the Egg Card commercials were aired in 1999 and these were built around the brand not recognising stereotypes and that all customers are viewed as individuals.

Since launch in 1998, the market has become fiercely competitive and Egg has had to reinforce its differentiation in the face of this. The third campaign aired in October 2000 relied less heavily on the promotion of products and ran a provocative campaign featuring Rob, the over-enthusiastic Egg employee who loves his customer, Stu so much and is prepared to go to ridiculous lengths to help him. The advertising was found to be both

memorable and polarising amongst consumers.

Egg also uses the national press extensively to continue to acquire and cross sell to its customer base with appropriate and motivating offers.

## Brand Values

Egg is built around a single ethos that its products and services are tailored to individuals. The brand's statement is at the core of its offer and summarises exactly what it aims to deliver to its customers: Egg is your groundbreaking partner, who is always there for you, offering simple, smart financial solutions.

Egg's brand values are: simple, transparent, mutually beneficial, empathetic, modern, fresh and liberating.

## Future Plans

Egg will continue to innovate and develop groundbreaking solutions to empower individuals to grow.

**www.egg.com**

# www.excite.co.uk

## Market Context

Despite the numerous dotcom failures, there is evidence to suggest that the outlook for Europe's internet market is still positive. Jupiter MMXI estimates that by 2005, 71.6 million Western European households will be online, or 43% of all households. The internet will thus establish itself as a major mass-market medium in Western Europe by 2005. Currently in the UK the number of people going online from home has risen by one million to 13.5 million over the five months from October 2000 to February 2001.

Portals remain the most familiar places on the internet. According to Jupiter MMXI (February 2001 UK Market) 78.9% of UK web users have visited a portal, compared with 53.1% who have visited entertainment sites or 31.2% who have tried news/information sites. The European portal market is broadly dominated by US portals and European telecommunications companies. Fifteen major players are competing in this market aiming to become the leading European portal.

## Achievements

In June 2000, Excite UK won the New Media Age Award for the Best Use of Wireless for Excite Mobile. Excite Mobile is a WAP portal that can be fully personalised with seamless interface to excite.co.uk web content. In Computer Active spring 2000 Web Guide, Excite UK was described as "possibly the most comprehensive source of information for business or leisure in the United Kingdom today."

In December 2000, Manchester United's

David Beckham, handed over a $25,000 cheque to the charity UNICEF, at the beginning of the clash between Manchester United and Ipswich at Old Trafford, courtesy of Excite UK Ltd.

## Key Management

Evan Rudowski is Managing Director of Excite Europe Ltd. He joined Excite in March of 1996 as the company's 45th employee. Before assuming his current post, he served in a variety of senior positions at the company's California headquarters, overseeing various product and business development activities.

A thirteen year veteran of internet and online services, Rudowski was previously Business Development Manager at News Corporation's iGuide internet venture in New York. He began his career at Times Mirror's Newsday and New York Newsday, where he helped launch and develop some of the earliest online newspaper efforts in the US.

Lorraine Thomson is Vice President, Commercial Operations of Excite Europe Ltd and is responsible for sales, production and brand marketing and development across the territory.

Lorraine joined Excite in July 2000 from Diageo plc where she had been Marketing Director for Burger King UK and Eire, and International Strategic Marketing Manager at Guinness.

Rebecca Miskin is General Manager for Excite UK Ltd, responsible for the growth and development of the Excite UK network. She joined Excite from IPC Media where she was Commercial Director, responsible for revenues and business development across IPC's digital brands.

Rebecca's responsibilities at IPC Media included Intellectual Property Director for IPC Magazines head office, Business Development Director and Commercial Director for IPC Electric, and International Publisher for IPC magazines.

## Background

On the evening of February 28 1993, six young Stanford university graduates decided to create a software tool to manage access to the vast amount of information available on the world wide web. By October 1995, these students launched the Excite suite of services in the US and within a year Excite was made public.

In May 1997 Excite Inc became one of the first search engines to address the need for locally relevant web searching by launching its European search network, Excite Europe. At the vanguard of this move was Excite UK Ltd which joined forces with a number of content providers to deliver information tailored to the needs of UK net users. Today excite.co.uk provides its visitors with a wealth of 'information channels' as well as a convenient starting point for general web surfing from multiple platforms, mobile and fixed.

Excite innovated with the launch of 'My Excite Start Page' – the first personalised web service in the UK – which responds to requirements of individuals – keeping them informed and entertained with relevant and personalised content which is matched to their specific interests.

On January 1 1999, BT bought a 50% share in Excite Inc subsidiary, Excite UK. On June 1 1999, Excite Inc completed its merger with @Home Network to become Excite@Home. This merger placed Excite at the forefront of the multi-device universe. Excite UK is a joint venture, now owned 58% by Excite@home and 42% by BT.

## Product/Service

Excite UK offers superior search and email facilities to over one million home internet users in the UK, making it the fifth most used portal in the UK (Source: MMXI February 2001). Part of one of the world's leading new media brands, Excite UK offers a personalised and content-rich starting point for both new and experienced internet users, together with one of the most comprehensive localised search facilities in the UK.

Amongst its highly customisable package of internet services, Excite

UK offers a personalised 'My Excite Start Page', free web based email, online shopping and access to eleven different information channels – including Computers, Entertainment & Games, Jobs & Careers, Lifestyle, Money, Mobile & WAP, Motoring, News, Sport and Travel. As a complementary platform to the PC-based services, Excite Mobile allows users to access personalised information from a WAP phone through www.mobile.excite.co.uk. Blue Mountain Arts (www.uk.bluemountain.com), the leading e-card greetings service (part of the Excite family of businesses) can also be accessed via Excite UK.

MANY ARE CALLED, FEW SUCCEED

OFFICIAL MOVIE

MANCHESTER UNITED

BEYOND THE PROMISED LAND

## Promotion

Excite was the first online portal to mount a major TV-led advertising campaign in the UK in March 1999 and has subsequently launched campaigns utilising TV, press, radio, outdoor and online. Excite's promotional objectives are to increase brand awareness, traffic and registrations and ultimately to achieve brand loyalty.

Its advertising aims to promote Excite as a clear, user-friendly site that lets users go quickly to the services required. Advertising communicates key messages about simplifying the internet showing that whatever your preferences you can get what you want from the internet at Excite. Furthermore, product specific messages promoting services such as free text messaging, free email and search facilities are also key.

A major new press and outdoor brand campaign was launched in October 2000 which saw a creative style reflecting the Excite logo itself. This was supported by an online Christmas promotion to drive brand switching. The promotion gave away some of the best prizes on the internet over the Christmas period.

Excite also invests in sponsorship activity having sponsored the Manchester United video/DVD 'Beyond the Promised Land' and the British street luge champion, Peter Eliot.

Also key to the promotional strategy is direct communication. Excite embarks on regular email newsletters to its base to keep them informed of latest developments and offers. This is especially important in light of the recent re-design of the Excite homepage to improve the service for users.

Through a dedicated and fun programme of trade and consumer public relations, Excite is also able to raise its profile amongst key audiences.

## Brand Values

Excite aims to provide a personalised daily starting point for everything you want from the web.

## Future Plans

Excite UK will continue to be a major player in the UK internet market enhancing the consumer experience through continuous product development and meeting consumer needs.

**www.excite.co.uk**

# Expedia.co.uk
## Everything for Travel

## Market Context

In the history of modern travel there have been three defining moments: the development of the jet engine which triggered the rapid mass movement of people; worldwide computerised booking engines allowing the rapid exchange of information; and most recently the internet which puts ordinary people in control of their travel arrangements for the first time.

Analysts say that the UK, one of the key European travel markets, is ready to embrace travel e-commerce with 63% of consumers believing that the internet will become the dominant technology for booking holidays within five years (Source: PhoCusWright The European Online Travel Marketplace 2000-2002 December 2000). In this environment Expedia.co.uk has established itself as the number one full service online travel company in the UK. The opportunities are huge with the online bookings market already worth $280 million in 1999 and set to reach $3.35 billion by 2003 (Source: Gartner Group).

## Achievements

Globally, Expedia is ranked in the top ten travel agents in the world through sales – counting both online and offline companies. The financial year ending in June 2000, saw Expedia Inc achieve gross bookings of US$1.325 billion for its four sites in the US, Canada, UK and Germany. In March 2001, Expedia Inc reported positive cash flow five quarters ahead of its March 2002 target.

In the UK, Expedia.co.uk has quickly built up a reputation for excellence of technology and consumer service, as its recent tally of awards testifies. It was voted Europe's best travel site by Forrester in The Best of Europe's E-commerce awards in August 1999, winner of Best Online Travel Site by

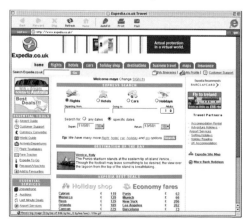

New Media Age Awards in 1999 and 2000, winner of Best Travel Information Service by the Telegraph Travel Awards, October 2000 and winner of Best Travel Site in the Future Internet Publishing Awards 2000.

## Key Management

James Vaile, Managing Director, has worked for Expedia.co.uk since November 1998, steering it

through its UK launch and the successful floatation of its parent company, Expedia Inc, on the Nasdaq stock exchange in November 1999. As MD he has overall responsibility for the management of the business including marketing, sales, supplier relationships and fulfilment operations.

The success of Expedia.co.uk means James plays a major role in promoting the company's successful e-travel model. He believes that the business needs to be exciting and fun and that online travel, a product at the cutting edge of today's business world, really is history in the making.

Nickie Smith, Marketing Manager has been in her current role since Expedia.co.uk's creation by Microsoft in November 1998. She is responsible for building awareness of the Expedia brand and service amongst consumers and small businesses, driving website registrations, improving conversion rates to sales through more targeted promotions and building customer loyalty through an active Customer Relationship Management (CRM) strategy.

Tim Hughes, Business Development Manager joined Expedia.co.uk in March 2000. Tim's responsibilities include management of distribution channels, development of new products, content acquisition and assessing strategic relationships.

Edward Hanrahan, Business Operations Manager, joined the Expedia UK team in 1999. Edward has responsibility for commercial relationships with travel suppliers and manages Expedia.co.uk's customer service and fulfilment operations.

## Background

Expedia made its debut on the internet with its US-based site, Expedia.com, on 22 October 1996. Launched by Microsoft, this represented the first foray into the online travel arena by a major technology player.

After several years of development, a specially tailored site for the UK market was introduced by MSN, Microsoft's consumer internet service, and Expedia.co.uk was born on 12 November 1998. It is now the number one online travel agent in the UK. Expedia.co.uk's parent group, Expedia Inc, floated on the Nasdaq stock exchange 10 November 1999 – Microsoft spun off around 17% of Expedia Inc for £78.2 million to raise capital

## Travel, Expedia's thought of everything. Have you?

■ FLIGHTS ■ HOTELS ■ CAR RENTAL ■ CITY GUIDES   Expedia.co.uk

for further development and marketing. Expedia.co.uk went on to become the first UK full service online travel company to launch an integrated wireless travel information product for both Personal Digital Assistants and WAP phones with the launch of Expedia To Go in December 2000.

## Product/Service

Expedia.co.uk gives customers the choice and control to easily plan their travel by allowing them access to exactly the same information as a high street travel agent. Users have the choice of booking from 450 airlines, more than 68,000 accommodation options with more than four million hotel rooms, the top 20 UK tour operators' package deals and car rental from all the major agencies. Its market position allows Expedia to negotiate significant exclusive discounts on accommodation and travel, with discounts of up to 70% on published hotel rates and up to 750,000 specially negotiated airfares on sale at any one time.

The site also includes related services such as photo processing, insurance and travel goods, in-depth destination guides and maps, a comprehensive travel information service with a free online newsletter, and thousands of useful links to relevant websites. Underpinning this is leading-edge security encryption, a comprehensive customer privacy policy and excellent customer care supported by a free helpline.

## Promotion

Expedia.co.uk has an innovative and comprehensive marketing strategy that embraces advertising, PR, sponsorship, promotions, online marketing and CRM.

In January 2000, Expedia.co.uk became the first online travel company to be promoted on UK television when it launched a £4 million integrated advertising campaign covering press, online advertising and PR. The theme was Hands On Travel For Hands On People.

The campaign was extended to Heathrow Airport in May 2000 where Expedia achieved another first for an online travel business by taking a premium and highly-visible outdoor advertising position. Other activity during the year long airport presence included Expedia-branded trolleys, advertising on the Heathrow underground platforms and branded luggage on carousels.

In January 2001, Expedia.co.uk's second TV and poster brand campaign was unveiled across TV, outdoor sites, press and online. The result was record sales and visitors to the site within days. Using the strapline Expedia.co.uk – When It Comes To Travel, We've Thought Of Everything, Have You? The campaign communicates how Expedia.co.uk takes care of every element of an individual's travel arrangements including flights, hotel and car hire

bookings as well as valuable information about the destination. However, the humour in the advertising reflects that some things are really down to the consumer.

Expedia again broke new ground when it became the official online travel agent for the British and Irish Lions rugby union team's tour of Australia in Summer 2001, selling tickets to the matches, together with associated flights, hotels, cars and tours. Expedia also sponsored Martin Johnson, England's second row Captain and leader of the last Lions team, to be the face of Expedia's on and offline marketing activity. And to give the team a boost during their tour Down Under, Expedia created its own cheerleader team – The Expedia Lionesses – consisting of seven women and a lone man picked from more than 400 hopefuls who travelled to Australia and lead the fans in song.

Expedia has also waged a campaign on behalf of the consumer to highlight the fact that despite working longer hours than the rest of Europe, Britain has the fewest bank holidays. An online petition attracted nearly 25,000 signatures while a second tranche of research released on 2 January 2001 revealed that the rest of Britain would like to have an official bank holiday after New Year's Day, as is already the case in Scotland, to help beat the back-to-work blues.

## Brand Values

Expedia.co.uk prides itself on caring for its customers' needs, by providing the level and depth of care and involvement they require for each trip. Expedia.co.uk offers every element of travel arrangements in one place to enable the customer to design the trip of their choice.

## Future Plans

Expedia.co.uk will focus on providing greater value for its customers through its Expedia Special Rate (ESR) properties. ESRs provide savings of up to 70% on the published price at selected hotels. The exclusively negotiated rooms are identifiable by a yellow bar on the site.

Expedia's technology will enable it to leverage its buying power, in order that customers will benefit from further discounts on an even wider range of products.

Expedia's CRM strategy will enable it to develop more relevant, personal and targeted relationships with its customers and to segment customers with a B2B and a B2C multi-strand product.

EXPEDIA LIONESS   www.Expedia.co.uk

**www.expedia.co.uk**

# eyestorm
## www.eyestorm.com

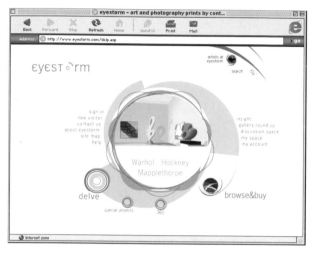

## Market Context

eyestorm is an arts media company which has been a significant pioneer of a new market: that of limited-edition artworks by well known artists at affordable prices. Prior to eyestorm's launch it was difficult to acquire a piece of art by a famous artist without spending thousands of pounds. eyestorm has opened up the exclusive world of art collecting to a much broader audience, creating a luxury brand out of the connoisseurial art world.

Traditionally, the art market has been fragmented and cloaked in mystery. Galleries can be intimidating and run along the policy that 'if you have to ask how much it is, you can't afford it'. The gallery art target market is small and elite. No site is comparable to eyestorm as it is the only one that holds exclusive agreements with the world's leading artists.

The eyestorm founders saw the gap in the market and secured the key asset – the artists, who they signed up on an exclusive basis for limited-edition artworks that are not sold anywhere else on the internet. The artists appreciated the idea as it gave them global exposure and the opportunity to reach a much wider audience than previously possible. The site also provides biographical information on the artists for consumers to explore before acquiring an artwork. Prices range from US$20 for a CD to over US$45,000 for an original piece of work. The average price is around $500.

## Achievements

eyestorm was launched in December 1999 and now showcases over 70 top name artists from all over the world including Jeff Koons, Damien Hirst, Helmut Newton, David Hockney, Marc Quinn, Ralph Gibson, Erwin Blumenfeld and Sebastião Salgado. eyestorm has also made strategic alliances with Magnum, the world-famous photographic agency, and The Saatchi Gallery. All the artists sign an exclusive agreement with eyestorm for their online limited-edition artworks. The company is the market leader in online contemporary and modern art in the UK and US in terms of both the quality and number of artists.

Within its first year the company raised US$25 million from investors such as Charles Schwab and NEA, received over five million hits per month and achieved US$ seven-figure revenue in the first eight months of trading.

The company has featured consistently in the press as a top online project, having featured in Forbes Best of the Web, The Sunday Times eLeague of top European Internet Ventures, and American Photo (Editor's Choice), amongst others.

eyestorm works with artists to help them support their charities. Examples are an online auction of a Damien Hirst original from which the proceeds went to the artist's charity, and the sale of a limited-edition book by Robert Del Naja, with proceeds going to The Red Cross.

## Key Management

Don Smith, CEO was previously Managing Director of Tony Stone Images, a subsidiary of Getty Images Inc, the world's leading stock photography business. During his tenure there, Don was responsible for the migration of the analogue, paper-based business onto a new website, and the repositioning of the Tony Stone Images brand. Prior to this, Don was company MD of Hulton Getty, Europe's leading supplier of archival stock photography. Additionally Don spent ten years in senior management positions within the print and reprographic industry.

David Grob, Founder and Head of Content has twenty years experience of owning and managing art galleries in London, Paris and Los Angeles. Key artists exhibited during this period include Brancusi, Calder, Moore, Picasso, Renoir and Warhol. Photographic artists exhibited include Kertesz, Helmut Newton, Man Ray, Stieglitz and Wegman. Between 1994

and 1996 David Grob was International Director of PaceWildenstein, managing the London and LA galleries. Throughout his career he has been successful in developing new artists, most recently Damien Hirst.

### Background

eyestorm was conceived in August 1999 by two art dealers David Grob and Michael Hue-Williams, with the backing of Arts Alliance and e-Partners. Don Smith joined as CEO to drive the business and build the team.

Key to the success of the company was securing the exclusive agreements with leading artists as this would secure the asset base. With names like Damien Hirst and David Hockney being among the first to join, it became easier for the artist liaison team to encourage other artists to showcase their work on the site.

The business has been grown from its offices in London, operating globally, but focusing on key markets in the UK and the US. In late 2000 offices opened in both New York and Paris.

The investor base was expanded to include Vertex, Charles Schwab and NEA as the company successfully completed its third round funding. This is seen as 'smart money' as eyestorm's investors provide not just funds but also networks of contacts and facilities which help grow the business.

### Product/Service

eyestorm is the leading luxury art brand selling limited-edition and original artwork by established artists. The work consists mainly of photographic prints, with a growing number of books, CDs and art objects. In addition, editorial and special projects such as topical online discussions also provide an educational resource for a growing number of people interested in contemporary art, culture and style.

### Promotion

Promotional activity has focused on combining offline activity such as brand advertising, advertorial and sales promotions with key online advertising and affiliate deals. PR is seen as being instrumental in positioning art in both a fashion and lifestyle context. eyestorm has sponsored major art events like the Apocalypse exhibition at the Royal Academy, and The Serpentine Gallery summer party. Other projects have involved a crossover into other related fields, for example hosting the online

architecture awards in collaboration with Tank magazine, and setting a fashion photography competition for students at Central St Martin's School of Art in London.

### Brand Values

eyestorm is dedicated to opening up the world of contemporary art to a wider global audience. eyestorm is a luxury brand bringing high-quality works by major artists within the reach of more people than ever before, and provides a continually evolving, interactive web space that is designed to attract, involve and inform a broad range of visitors. The company pushes the boundaries of art, commerce and technology, providing a platform for artists, and a resource for art-appreciators.

### Future Plans

At its inception, the bulk of eyestorm's business consisted of selling photographic artwork to individuals over the internet. The company now has four distinct business units which will be grown through 2001: Lifestyle – focusing on B2C sales to individuals, Art Services – working in the specialist art market with low-edition and unique works, and special commissions, Corporate Art – selling to leading corporate clients and Licensing and commissioning services – bringing companies and artists together.

The company is also moving into bricks and mortar to complement its online activities. Its first art showrooms have already opened in Paris and London, and there are plans to open showrooms in New York and San Francisco between 2001 and 2002. As well as forging new relationships, eyestorm will expand its selection of available works by nurturing and developing existing relationships with artists and partners such as Magnum Photos and The Saatchi Gallery.

The company is also looking at expanding its operation into Asia, using investor Vertex to assist with the contacts and strategy.

**www.eyestorm.com**

# FinanceWise

|||||||||||||||||||||||||||||||

## Market Context

The internet has brought us the concept of easy access to all the information you could ever want at the click of a mouse. However, while the information has been available it has not always been easy to find. Search engines and directories therefore have developed to help web users to find what they want on the net. Testament to the usefulness of search engines and directories is that they have become some of the most successful sites on the web enabling millions of people each day to locate their interests among the many billions of pages published on the web. Current estimates suggest that the web grows by 7.3 million pages per day.

Search engines allow the web to fulfil its promise to internet users – the delivery of the location with the correct content to the searcher whether for entertainment, education, product or services. As the amount of information available has grown, the number of search engines and directories has mushroomed correspondingly, with increasing specialisation catering for specific interests and niche audiences.

As a specialist search engine and directory FinanceWise has been developed to serve the particular needs of those who work in the financial markets.

## Achievements

FinanceWise has received many awards and accolades including 'site of the day' from Yahoo! as well as a finalist for Business Website of the Year from The Financial Times. Other acknowledgements include designated 'hot site' by USA Today plus inclusion in The Scout Report's Business and Economics Selection.

## Key Management

Henry Perks, Publisher FinanceWise, has overseen the development of FinanceWise from its inception and launch through to the present day.

Toby Charkin, Editor FinanceWise, joined FinanceWise in 2001 as a specialist editor with previous experience of developing search engine content and functionality.

## Background

FinanceWise was developed to provide the financial industry with the fastest and most effective means of accessing all areas of banking and financial information from the internet free of charge. It was a logical development for a specialist financial publishing house that understood the type of information the financial market required and

FinanceWise
||||||||||||||||||||||||||
www.financewise.com
makes the w.w.w. of difference

FinanceWise - the revolutionary Web
search engine for banking and finance
professionals

had the capabilities to deliver the information in the appropriate format.

Initial research showed that the industry was impressed by the amount and diverse nature of information that was available on the web. However in most cases there was disappointment at how long it took to find what they wanted. FinanceWise's target audience of banking and finance professionals operate within a business environment that has enormous time pressures so the time taken to find what they wanted was of particular concern. Many stated that the difficulties associated with searching through the many thousands of results returned by general search sites made the web impractical for regular use. They pointed out that relevant web links were buried amongst irrelevant matches to their specific search. These incorrect topic returns were often the result of specific financial terms having other meanings within a wider context: for example, a search on 'bonds' would return family bonds, glue bonds and James Bonds.

To address this FinanceWise filters the user's web search to deliver 100% banking and finance content. By indexing only sites and pages relevant to the world of banking and finance, it takes users straight to the information that is relevant to their work. It helps visitors to bypass the millions of megabytes of irrelevant data that is returned with non subject-specific search engines.

Today FinanceWise has expanded its range of services for those within its target market covering recruitment, news and conferences whilst maintaining its aim of delivering visitors the information they want in the shortest possible time.

## Product/Service

Unlike general search engines, which often only skim the top few layers of a website, FinanceWise's niche-specific focus means all the available pages within a relevant website are indexed. Users can therefore rely on FinanceWise to deliver the most comprehensive, in-depth source of financial information available on the web. It has indexed over 4,000 sites offering the user more than 3.5 million searchable documents.

FinanceWise offers three types of search option. Users can search by keyword; by specific classes of products, suppliers, information or companies; as well as by industry sector listings and by topic – enabling the search to be focused according to the nature of the query. A user can choose the most appropriate line of searching, and because each site is reviewed by an editorial team before being allowed entry into the database, the user can get an independent summary of the link before visiting a site.

Even with the best technology, the very nature of search engines means that the information sought is often located in a broad cross section of categories. Special reports have therefore been developed to bring all the information together in one convenient resource enhanced by topic-specific editorial abstracts for each site. Each report contains links to hundreds of relevant sites, hundreds of articles from leading industry magazines and content from industry participants. FinanceWise visitors can therefore choose to search their particular segment of the financial markets from the part of the site that best matches their interests. In this way FinanceWise has done the hard work for our users.

FinanceWise is more than just a search engine and specialist directory – it offers visitors a range of features that encourage them to spend longer on the site and to visit more often. A finance-specific bookshop is featured and a financial conference and training search facility provide details on events globally. A powerful job search contains thousands of vacancies within the financial sectors worldwide.

## Promotion

The initial launch campaign of FinanceWise set out to increase traffic and awareness of the site by promoting the following points: a free service specifically for the banking and finance professional; the delivery of a filtered set of search results that excluded non-financial information; and a site that was quick and easy to use. Target groups included those with English as their first language and countries with the largest numbers of people online.

As part of the Risk Waters Group, FinanceWise had access to all of the group's in-house products and publications to reach the financial markets as well as public relations and direct mail campaigns. The campaigns ran in the financial media including the Financial Times, the Economist and the Wall Street Journal and were included both on and offline. The best results however were achieved via the direct mail campaign.

FinanceWise has most effectively reached its audience through smaller niche websites that provide a more concentrated focus on its target groups. It has been

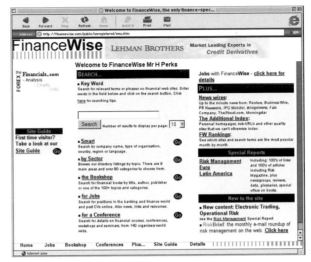

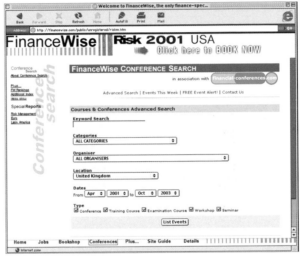

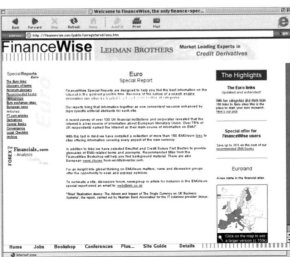

successful at generating traffic by encouraging sites selected for special reports and top tens to display linking buttons and awards. Those sites indexed by FinanceWise have exactly the right audience for its functionality.

## Brand Values

FinanceWise provides banking and finance professionals with the fastest route to the information they want on the web. It aims to be a comprehensive and authoritative tool, combining powerful technology with a human editorial overview.

## Future Plans

Following the success of the special reports on risk management, Latin America, and the Euro, FinanceWise plans to launch several new special reports covering areas such as Asia, energy and weather, financial IT, and telecommunications. It also aims to enhance its news coverage, particularly in these topic-specific areas.

As well as new content areas, FinanceWise is always looking to improve the functionality of the site, by adding polls and surveys for its community of users, and providing users with featured interactive tools and reports.

The search will also be expanded to cover new areas. FinanceWise is looking to work with strategic partners in order to cover areas such as reference material and journal articles, so that it can provide a comprehensive choice of search facilities for those involved in the financial markets.

FinanceWise is constantly evolving and improving in order to keep pace with our users' requirements, and as the amount of information available on the web continues to expand FinanceWise will become more and more essential to its users.

**www.financewise.com**

**macromedia®**
**FLASH PLAYER™**

## Market Context

The internet is a constantly evolving medium and the possibilities of what can be done with it change with every day. For the people who develop and design web content, it is essential to have tools which help them expand these horizons – pushing the envelope of the web's capabilities. For website owners, it is vital to deliver the best possible experience for users, in order to build loyalty and keep them coming back for more.

Flash Player is one of the most important technologies available for delivering this experience, as Macromedia Flash empowers web designers, programmers and rich media developers to build engaging, next generation web experiences. Other advanced web design formats, like Dynamic HTML and Java compete with Flash Player, but are not compatible with as many browsers. Macromedia has the added advantage over other web development tools by being free of design restrictions, allowing it to be used in ways that precisely fit every requirement.

## Achievements

Macromedia, the company that owns Flash Player, has built it into one of the web's pre-eminent brands. Such is its popularity and widespread use, that Macromedia Flash has become the de facto standard for creating web animation and simple interactivity. Macromedia is a powerhouse in this market, with over 75% of web developers – more than a million people – using one or more of its products.

The Macromedia Flash Player is believed to be the most downloaded web software, with more than 220 million users able to view its high impact, bandwidth-friendly content. It attracts over 1.4 million downloads daily, allowing 90% of all web users to view Flash content.

Flash Player is pre-installed in most web browsers and on most computers. It is included in Apple Macintosh and Windows 98 operating systems as well as AOL and Netscape Navigator.

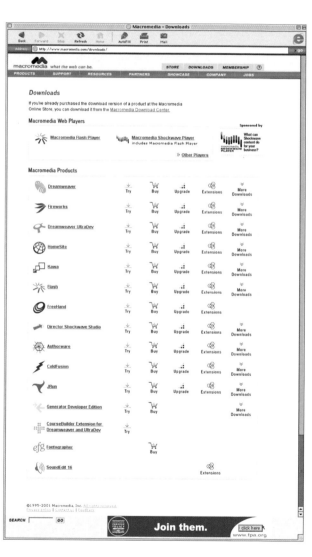

The software has been laden with awards. Examples of awards given to the latest version, Macromedia Flash 5, include: Macworld Editors' Choice Award for Best Web Motion Software; MacUser Award for Best Interactive Media and Web Techniques Editors' Choice Design Tool Award.

## Key Management

Rob Burgess is Chairman and CEO of Macromedia Inc, the company that created and owns Macromedia Flash and the Flash Player. Under Burgess' tenure, Macromedia has grown from a CD-Rom-based multimedia company into the leader in the web publishing market. Prior to joining Macromedia, Burgess worked extensively in the world of high-performance computer graphics, with experience in key executive posts at Silicon Graphics and Alias Research.

Kevin Lynch is President of Macromedia Products. Lynch joined Macromedia in 1996 and has been instrumental in forming Macromedia's

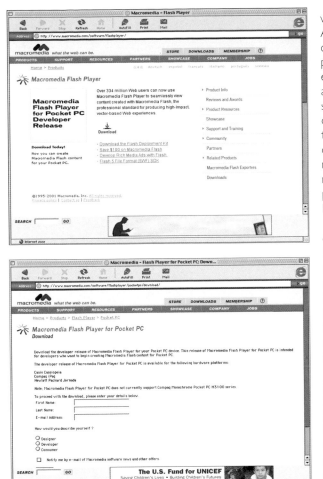

web strategy. Aiming to create practical, powerful, and enjoyable web authoring solutions, he defined and led the development of Dreamweaver, now the market-leading professional HTML editor.

As President of Products, Lynch is responsible for developing Macromedia's award-winning family of software and solutions.

Prior to joining Macromedia, Lynch was Director of General Magic's operating system and applications teams, where he pioneered a navigational user interface for handheld communicators. Previously, he worked at Frame Technology, where he designed the user interface and developed the first Macintosh release of FrameMaker in 1989, and then led the development of FrameMaker across platforms as manager of Frame's Core Technology Group.

## Background

Macromedia, the company behind Flash Player, is a US$250 million software company based in San Francisco with more than 1000 employees. It has been recognised as both a Fortune e-50 and a USA Today e-Business 50 company.

## Product/Service

Macromedia Flash is the key to designing and delivering low-bandwidth animations, presentations and websites. It offers scripting capabilities and server-side connectivity for creating engaging applications, web interfaces and training courses.

With Macromedia Flash, users can create animation, interactivity, and scalability but still keep file sizes small enough to stream across a normal modem connection. For example, a three minute animated movie, complete with sound, can take up just 191KB, allowing it to be easily streamed and shared without taking a long time to download.

Flash Player displays web application 'front ends' – such as interactive online advertising, animation, and website user interfaces. It is different from Macromedia Shockwave Player, in that Shockwave displays 'destination' web content, such as high-performance games, interactive product simulations and online entertainment.

## Promotion

As Flash Player is pre-installed in most web browsers and new PCs, it has a ready-made distribution network and marketing platform. It is also in the fortunate and enviable position of being required for websites that have been design using Flash software.

Flash 5 Player Installer

An ever increasing proportion of websites use Flash and many lead their visitors to the Macromedia site to download the latest version of it if visitors don't already have it. Macromedia distributes and markets the software through the main Macromedia website as well as through its alliances with key partners, such as Microsoft, Netscape and AOL.

## Brand Values

The mission of Macromedia and the core value of Flash Player is to make work easier for people who build web content and to enable them to deliver the most effective user experiences. Flash is all about creation and empowerment – inspiring and enabling designers to create compelling web content.

Flash expands horizons by opening up new possibilities for designers, and, by being available so widely, is committed to openness and flexibility. It is the web's design standard.

## Future Plans

The evolution of the internet into mobile devices – such as phones and personal digital assistants – is an obvious area of expansion for Macromedia and Flash. The release of Flash Player for the Pocket PC platform will enable developers to tune their content for mobile devices. A fuller version of the Pocket PC Flash Player will soon be introduced.

**www.macromedia.com**

# flutter.com

Bet on on one.
More cash.
More fun.

Find out more

FREE
£10 flutter
JOIN NOW!

## Market Context

The online gaming entertainment market is estimated at £2,000 billion globally. The online betting market in the UK is estimated to be worth £750 million and includes such brands as Ladbrokes, William Hill and Blue SQ. flutter.com is a unique consumer idea that seeks to deliver better value for punters and make betting more entertaining. It therefore may be seen to compete not just in the online betting market but also in the online entertainment market.

## Achievements

flutter.com is acknowledged to be the UK's leading person-to-person betting site. By January 2001, over 400,000 flutters had taken place. It has been warmly received by the business and marketing communities – shown both by the raising of £25 million capital in May 2000 from companies such as Europ@web, UBS Capital, Chase Episode 1, Index Ventures and Benchmark Capital as well as the positive press it has received since launch. Red Herring has credited it as 'the brightest star in London' and Fortune magazine stated it was 'the eBay of betting'. flutter.com was also selected to be a finalist for Revolution's award for 'Most Innovative Online Business of 2000'.

## Key Management

Prior to founding flutter.com, Josh Hannah, Co-President, worked in the private equity practice of the management consulting firm Bain & Co leading a new venture generation initiative focused on identifying and funding new business concepts. Josh has an MBA from Stanford University and a BA from the University of California, Berkeley.

Josh's choice of flutter would be that Microsoft will relocate from Seattle one hour away to Canada to escape US anti-trust prosecution.

Vince Monical, Co-Founder and Co-President, was a founding member of the e-commerce practice at Bain & Co in San Francisco. There he worked with Silicon Valley venture capitalists helping them make internet investments and worked with their portfolio companies to refine their strategies. He was also an integral part of the technology practice at Andersen Consulting where he led technology efforts for five fortune 500 companies. He holds an MBA from Wharton and a BS from the University of Illinois.

Vince's choice of flutter would be that Al Gore will be the next US president in 2004.

Prior to joining flutter.com, Alice Avis, VP Marketing and Content, was the Global Brand Director for Johnnie Walker, a leading global brand with sales in excess of £500 million worldwide. She has extensive entrepreneurial experience as a former Managing Director at Cutler and Gross. Alice has an MBA from INSEAD and an MA from Cambridge University. She also worked at Bain & Co in the UK.

Alice's choice of flutter would be on the FTSE. Any day you like.

## Background

Founders Josh and Vince had a bet at their Superbowl Party in 1999. Josh lost on that occasion, but looking for an opportunity to get the better of Vince, he proposed a new bet via email. The two kept challenging each other head-to-head with friends joining in and so before long they were developing a website to enable others to take part in the fun of person-to-person betting.

Josh and Vince decided to launch flutter.com in the UK to leverage the UK's global reputation as the centre of bookmaking excellence and to build a powerful team from amongst the innovative, entrepreneurial net community in London.

flutter.com was launched in April 2000 with a promotion around the Grand National, with the main site following immediately afterwards. Since then the flutter.com site has

**YOU CAN SET YOUR OWN ODDS SO, WHEN YOU WIN, YOU CAN WIN MORE**

BOOKIE FREE BETTING

**flutter.com**

BET ONE ON ONE MORE CASH MORE FUN

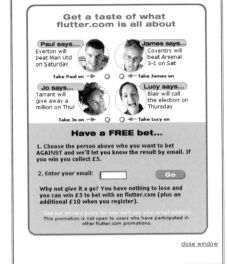

flutter.com makes its money from taking a 2.5% commission on the stakes of all evens bets and a 5% commission on the winnings of all other odds bets.

## Promotion

flutter.com's visual equity has been designed to help communicate clearly what the site does and to be welcoming to both traditional as well as novice punters alike. Hence gone are the old complicated betting language and dull feel of traditional bookmaking sites and in its place fun, provocative text and graphics.

From launch to early 2001 flutter.com ran two advertising campaigns. The first was targeted at traditional punters with the objective of convincing them they could get the best value bets at flutter.com.

The second campaign was targeted at City professionals and combines the 'More Cash' element of flutter.com's positioning with the 'More Fun' part. This was executed via a provocative advertising campaign, designed to provoke City workers to come and have a flutter.

## Brand Values

Like all wholly new concepts, flutter.com required a crystal clear brand positioning at launch. For flutter.com the winning positioning was 'Bet one-on-one. More Cash. More Fun'. Research showed this positioning most clearly communicated what flutter.com does and the benefits in it for consumers.

flutter.com offers punters two benefits. Firstly, it aims to offer the best value betting to punters on the net. Punters, it asserts, get better value because they can set their own odds and because the high commercial costs of running a commercial bookmakers such as shops, salaries and high profit margin have been cut out. This means that when punters win at flutter.com, they can win more money.

Secondly, players get the entertainment benefit of becoming members of a betting community. Players get to create their own bets, to wind up rival punters and fans via e-mail and have the chance to build online rivalries so that not only are they betting on the outcome of a match but also against a competitor.

been constantly upgraded based on users opinion of what they liked and what they didn't.

Whilst some of the topics punters have chosen to flutter on are predictable such as football and horse racing; highlights for 2000 also included Big Brother which at one point had more flutters on it than football and the world chess championships.

## Product/Service

flutter.com brings together thousands of online punters and fans to have a bet against each other. They can either take a bet another fan has already posted on the site or they can create a new one themselves.

To create a new bet, punters simply go to the site area of their choice and fill out a three step form. They choose their desired outcome, the odds they think are fair and enter the money they want to flutter. Their flutter is then posted on the site for other punters to see, disagree with and so be taken.

To guarantee payment, funds are held by the Royal Bank of Scotland for the duration of the flutter. Punters must have enough money in their accounts to cover the bet – and then these monies are held until such time as the bet outcome is known.

## Future Plans

flutter.com will continue to innovate in the online space. It plans at least one major initiative in 2001-2002. Additionally, it intends to deliver a whole succession of upgrades to the main flutter.com site as it continues to develop ideas centred around its users feedback.

**www.flutter.com**

## Market Context

Today's mobile telecommunications industry continues to grow at a rapid pace. In many countries mobile telephony subscriber growth has outpaced that of fixed line subscribers. In Europe, where the penetration of mobile

subscribers is high and SMS messaging has become the defacto standard for mobile data communication, the potential market for more sophisticated mobile internet services is huge.

Genie, BT's mobile internet division, was developed specifically to address the opportunity for the convergence of internet and mobile technologies and the growing demand for mobile lifestyle services. In this new and growing market Genie's total offer of global integration of fixed and mobile portals, as well as a fully online mobile phone sales business, competes with a wide range of the world's largest mobile telecommunications and web companies – AOL, NTT DoCoMo, Orange, Vodafone and Vizzavi and Yahoo! to name but a few.

With the advent of infrastructure improvements like GPRS and eventually G3, as well as technological improvements like colour browsers, billing and location based services as well as unified, instant and photo messaging, Genie stands to make major contributions to improvements to the consumer mobile internet experience that will be lasting and significant.

## Achievements

Genie has won several awards for its innovative services, including the Comdex m-commerce innovation award in 2000. Genie's web and wireless internet content and service partner list includes some of the biggest and best players on the internet such as Amazon, AOL, Bloomberg, British Airways, E4, Excite Sport, Freeserve, Guardian Unlimited, MSN, MTV,

TD Waterhouse and Yahoo!. Key infrastructure partners include Openwave Systems, with whom Genie and device partners such as Siemens will bring the first graphics-based browsers and developer application program interface (API) to the European mobile portal market.

In March 2001 Genie registered over four million unique visitors globally to the Genie web portals as well as driving substantial traffic, both in the fixed and mobile environments, generating 63 million web page impressions globally and 89 million WAP page impressions in that month.

By April 2001 Genie had established its position as Europe's leading mobile internet portal. Expanding its reach to over seven countries and serves over four million registered users worldwide – the largest user base for a multi-national, multi-language integrated mobile internet business.

## Key Management

Kent Thexton, prior to his recent appointment as President, was Managing Director. Since his appointment to this role in March 2000, he has overseen Genie's transformation from a UK mobile ISP to a leading global web and WAP portal with a clear vision of providing 'lifestyle services for a mobile generation'.

Prior to Kent's role at Genie, he was Marketing Director at BT Cellnet for nearly two years. In that time, he was instrumental in the re-branding of the business and the launch of BT Cellnet's pre-pay proposition. During his time at BT Cellnet, the pre-pay subscriber base grew to over four million active customers.

Will Harris, Vice President of Global Marketing, formerly Global Marketing Director, is responsible for the development of the Genie brand globally and for overall marketing activity and branding of Genie. Will was formerly a board director at Abbott Mead Vickers BBDO, where he directed critically acclaimed campaigns for Genie and BT Cellnet.

Previously, Will was a Director at WCRS for five years where he was notably responsible for the highly successful Orange brand-building campaign.

Laurence Alexander was appointed UK Managing Director of Genie in September 2000. He is responsible for consolidating and building on Genie's development in the UK and spearheads the introduction of new content and services to the marketplace. Prior to joining Genie, Laurence was Managing Director of consumer services for World Online where he oversaw and directed the

successful launch of World Online into the British market, as well as ensuring its positioning and branding remained consistent and successful.

## Background

Genie (www.genie.co.uk) was launched in March 1999 as BT Cellnet's mobile ISP. In October of that year, Genie announced a deal with Phone.com (now Openwave) to supply the WAP software platform to provide mobile internet services, such as email and access to a range of news, entertainment, sports, travel and banking services from its WAP phones.

2000 had many significant developments for the brand. In January WAP services launched through Genie and BT Cellnet became fully operational, open and commercially available. In April Genie became established as a wholly owned subsidiary of BT with the objective of becoming an international business and a market leader in the provision of quality internet content to any device, fixed or mobile, anywhere at anytime.

In September Genie and Yahoo! Europe joined forces to allow Yahoo! UK and Ireland's WAP content services accessible via the Genie portal. Further agreements with AOL and MSN followed later that year.

Genie continued to increase its international footprint in October with its mobile internet services in Italy through Infinito and the development of its mobile internet services in Spain and France.

In November GenieMobile™, the UK's first exclusively online mobile phone service was launched. It offers free mobile internet and text messaging and WAP services, as well as online mobile phone sales and customer care.

Genie and BT Cellnet announced the intention to offer wireless data access services to enterprises via seven's global network platform.

## Product/Service

Genie brings together the latest internet and mobile technology. It delivers personalised news and information via computer and mobile phone, giving users flexibility and choice over what they read and where they read it. With a range of services including email, text messaging and mobile internet access and content, Genie is the UK's market leading mobile internet provider.

GenieMobile™ provides online mobile phone sales, customer support and services. Launched in November 2000, it is also the UK's first exclusively online mobile service offering mobile phones with free internet and text messaging. It also provides 24-hour e-care and online billing.

As Genie users become more familiar with using mobile services, traffic patterns have begun to shift from being predominantly communications oriented to also include games, diversions and phone-centric applications. Examples of popular services have been Wireless pets, the new WAP virtual pet game from Digital Bridges, which has already enjoyed 29,000 downloads and 77,000 games played in only two weeks. Other highly popular, revenue-generating services include downloadable icons and ring tones, the popular Ladbrokes interactive betting service, and other highly viral games and diversions.

## Promotion

Much of Genie's initial promotional activity has focused on online and below-the-line advertising and promotion with some above-the-line press and radio executions supporting the launch of GenieMobile™ in November/December 2000.

March 2001 saw the launch of a major brand communications initiative, with TV, press and online campaigns. A TV campaign on national satellite and London terrestrial TV supported three executions promoting the Genie message of providing mobile internet services. The creative executions were developed to highlight a central brand message that Genie aims to provide alternatives to the norm and solutions that 'simplify life'. Three executions also ran in national press weekend supplements and selected lifestyle magazines, throughout March. Follow up activity promoted individual services and GenieMobile™.

## Brand Values

Genie is about challenging the status quo and providing useful and inspirational services for a mobile generation. It is about humanising technology and providing products and services that benefit the customer wherever they are, whenever they want, whatever network they are on.

## Future Plans

Genie is pursuing an international rollout program in other countries in Europe and Asia Pacific for both its web and WAP portals. Plans for the next generation of mobile services using GPRS and G3 are in progress.

**www.genie.co.uk**

# GOJObsite

## Market Context

The internet has rapidly become the first choice recruitment medium. According to Fletcher Research, more ABC1 job hunters use the internet for recruitment information than use either a broadsheet newspaper or their industry media. In 1999 in the UK alone, £24 million was spent recruiting candidates via third party recruitment sites, a figure that rose dramatically in 2000.

The potential rewards of this rapidly expanding market have led to an influx of recruitment sites, with at least 300 operating in the UK at the start of 2001. This has made online recruitment one of the most competitive sectors of the UK internet industry – with multi million pound advertising budgets being spent in the quest for number one status in the critical multi-sector market. Key brands in this market include the US giant Monster, the high spending Stepstone, the Guardian Media Group's Workthing and Reed.co.uk – the online offshoot of the high street recruitment agency network.

## Achievements

GoJobsite has consistently been placed in the top 40 of private internet companies in Europe (Sunday Times e-League). During 2000, Independent Internet Recruitment Surveys such as RMSMediaTech/Online Recruitment (March), RMSMediaTech Candidate Pool Analysis (May) and Riley/Recruitnet (August/September) voted the brand as Best Performing Site judged on criteria including number of visitors and candidates, cost, speed, usability and marketing.

GoJobsite is the only UK recruitment site to reach over 1% of the UK's digital media audience in both the MMXI International April 2000 and September 2000 surveys.

## Key Management

Keith Potts, Managing Director and Founder, migrated from his position as Managing Director of Pinnacle Internet services, an internet development company, into the MD role at GoJobsite in 1998.

Keith has grown the company turnover by over 600% and the staff headcount from fifteen to around 180 people. Keith has a software engineering background and continues to play a strategic role in the development of the product and the future direction and strategy of the company.

Since 1982 Graham Potts, now Director of IT, has played a key role in a range of high profile IT projects around the world, including building Nimrod fighter aircraft navigation systems, the Madrid stock exchange trading software and Eurostar Departure Control Systems. Graham is an expert in online transaction processing and database management and built the core search facility around which GoJobsite operates.

Dr Nick Lutte, Business Development Director and Chairman, is an experienced business strategist. Nick was instrumental in the deal that brought together Manpower and GoJobsite. Nick's business career began as Computer Simulation Lecturer at Manchester University, from where he undertook consultancy work including the design of the weapons guidance system for a high performance fighter. He later rose to become MD of Eurotherm, successfully masterminding its global expansion before, in 1995, meeting Keith Potts, investing in Pinnacle Internet, and playing a key role in the expansion of GoJobsite.

Chris Newson has served as GoJobsite's Marketing Director since 1998 and has a background in marketing and IT on an international level. Under Chris's guidance GoJobsite has established a position as the leading UK recruitment site. He has overseen increases in turnover from £100,000 to £1 million per month, and increases in traffic from 3,000 to 35,000 unique visitors per day. Chris has also been instrumental in GoJobsite's international expansion and the development of GoJobsite's new electronic recruitment services.

## Background

The market-leading GoJobsite is the UK's longest established multi-sector electronic recruitment service. It was founded as Jobsite in 1995 by three brothers – Keith, Graham and Eric Potts – as a product of their respective expertise in the fields of the internet, IT and recruitment. Jobsite was designed to use the latest technology in matching up job hunters and recruiters.

The company grew rapidly, proved to be highly effective, remained profitable and was at the forefront of introducing new job hunter services such as Jobs-by-Email and the MyJobsite personalised candidate home page – that would in time become industry standard.

Word of mouth recommendation ran at high levels and Jobsite quickly became one of the key UK internet brands and one of the UK's busiest sites. Recruiters received numerous responses from the site and vacancy numbers rocketed.

In January 2000, the world's largest staffing services company, Manpower Inc, was attracted to the strength of the Jobsite brand and invested in the company, in a deal that ensured Jobsite's operational independence. With Manpower's funding, the next step was to replicate Jobsite's success in Europe. To do this, the company needed a new brand and domain name. 'GoJobsite' was chosen after painstaking research, and the transition from Jobsite was carefully managed to minimise any negative effects on either the brand or site performance.

In November 2000, the GoJobsite site network was launched with national sites launched for the France, Germany, Ireland, Italy, Spain and UK.

The transition proved successful, with the keystone UK site's traffic hitting record levels by the start of 2001.

## Product/Service

GoJobsite offers a cutting edge electronic recruitment service that brings together excellent companies and strong candidates. It has consistently topped independent performance surveys in the online recruitment market.

GoJobsite advertises hundreds of thousands of jobs a month from across 35 industry sectors, with clients including IBM, Cable & Wireless, Nokia, Microsoft and Sony as well as many of Europe's leading recruitment agencies, including Computer Futures, Elan, Michael Page International and Robert Walters. Recruiters are given full access to one of the internet's best customer support services, with dedicated consultants providing advice and guidance on maximising responses to online vacancies.

Candidates register free of charge, post their CV onto the database, receive a daily match of jobs to their email inbox, and read in-depth career development articles.

At the core of GoJobsite's service is a fast and accurate search function housed in an intuitive award winning site and operating system that has been kept simple and uncluttered to maximise ease of search and navigation.

## Promotion

GoJobsite's promotional strategy has been highly successful in driving registrations to areas of highest client demand and outperforming competitors with far greater promotional budgets. GoJobsite's online promotional strategy is based on the company's in-depth understanding of the behaviour of internet users

HOW **LONG DO YOU WANT TO WAIT TO BECOME THE BOSS?**

www.jobsite.co.uk The fast way to a better job.

and uses one of internet's most effective online marketing operations to maintain consistently high traffic levels. These have made GoJobsite the only recruitment site to hold a top three position in all of MMXI Europe's usage surveys in 2000.

GoJobsite also employs highly targeted industry and skill-specific tactical campaigns developed in close partnership with clients and with GoJobsite's sales teams.

Offline, GoJobsite has employed targeted award winning advertising and a usage of ambient media that has earned widespread acclaim from the new media, advertising and recruitment industries.

A heavy focus on effective PR has led to coverage levels that beat GoJobsite's top competitors combined, helping to firmly differentiate the brand and its values in a crowded marketplace.

## Brand Values

The strength of the GoJobsite brand is very much rooted in its ability to deliver quality results for both candidates and recruiters. To achieve this, GoJobsite has placed a premium on developing highly intelligent approaches to meeting needs in areas of information technology, marketing and wider recruitment support. Additionally, GoJobsite has always committed to a partnership approach to its users on both sides of the recruitment equation.

For registered candidates this has meant a heavy focus on confidentiality and close involvement of job hunters in developing new services as well as carefully balancing the ratio of candidates to vacancies. For recruiters it has meant adopting a highly consultative approach based on an in-depth understanding of recruiting through the internet.

GoJobsite is heavily committed to raising the standard of business practice. It was a founder of the AOLR (Association of Online Recruiters) and continues to drive the industry forward through representation on the AOLR's Executive Committee.

## Future Plans

GoJobsite now aims to lead the European market for electronic recruitment solutions and to lengthen the relationships it enjoys with both candidates and recruiters.

To achieve this GoJobsite will remain at the forefront of exploiting new communications channels to supplement its internet and mobile phone services. It will also develop industry leading content and functionality services for candidates and recruiters.

The soft launch of its European site network will be developed in accordance with market requirements in key European countries, and new markets will be entered by the end of 2001.

**www.gojobsite.co.uk**

# interactive investor international
™

## Market Context

Mirroring the explosion in general web usage, there has been a surge in the number of people accessing financial information online. To meet this burgeoning demand, increasing numbers of providers, ranging from traditional high street banks and building societies through to internet start ups, have launched financial services. In this highly competitive market, consumers now have access to millions of web pages dedicated to financial products including mortgages, pensions, ISAs, equities, investment funds, savings insurance and credit cards.

interactive investor international (Interactive Investor) (www.iii.co.uk), was founded in 1995 and is now one of the leading personal finance sites in the UK, enabling its users to execute transactions online. Since spring 2000 it has been listed on the London Stock Exchange and Nasdaq and has a clear strategic plan which aims to transform more of its account holders into transactors. The business model based entirely on the provision of content has undergone considerable change – the need to generate income is a clear business imperative.

## Achievements

Since its launch in August 1995, Interactive Investor has been one of the leading online personal finance sites in the UK. With over 1.1 million registered account holders it has, at its peak, attracted in excess of 93.5 million page impressions per month (March 2000 Audited: ABC Electronic). In recognition of its unique service, Interactive Investor has been awarded a series of accolades, including commendations for specific financial products and its overall quality of service.

It was ranked as the top UK and European website in a survey of the twenty leading global financial information portals (Source: Lafferty Internet Ratings, January 2000). In a survey conducted by Morgan Stanley Dean Witter (August 1999), Interactive Investor was selected as one of the top five financial websites in Europe.

Media sponsored awards have also recognised the quality of Interactive Investor's service. The Financial Times, The Sunday Times and the Wall Street Journal Europe have all recognised its expertise, with the latter stating that Interactive Investor is: "The best website for investors in Europe."

These awards have come with good reason. For over five years, Interactive Investor has empowered users to identify, compare, monitor and buy online an ever-growing range of financial products. A measure of its reputation is the fact that Interactive Investor can count leading internet brands, AOL UK, Excite UK, Yahoo!Finance and Netscape, amongst its strategic partners. Thanks to its partnerships with BT Genie and NTL:, Interactive Investor's service is also available through WAP enabled mobile phones and digital interactive television. Interactive Investor has built a successful business by demystifying investment products and simplifying financial decisions.

## Key Management

Sherry Coutu, Chairman, founded interactive investor international in

1995. Prior to this she co-founded Internet Securities, a database company that provides emerging market securities information research via the internet. Sherry was a member of the financial services practice of Andersen Consulting (now Accenture) from 1987 to 1989 and Coopers & Lybrand (now PriceWaterhouseCooper) from 1989 to 1991. Sherry also serves as a Non-Executive Director of RM plc, a leading supplier of software, computer services and systems to schools and colleges in the UK, and is a director of the Public Records Office.

Tomás Carruthers, Chief Executive Officer joined the group in August 1997 and has served in his current role since March 1999. Prior to his appointment as CEO, Tomás founded and served as Managing Director of interactive investor solutions, a wholly owned subsidiary of interactive investor international plc, as well as Business Development Director of the group. From September 1994 to July 1997, Tomás helped start and was Business Development Director of Electronic Share Information, now the UK subsidiary of E*Trade.

Candice Hodgson is Head of Corporate Communications. She spent four years in the financial marketing industry, which included the position of Senior

Brand Manager at Investec Group in Johannesburg from December 1994 to September 1998. Candice joined interactive investor international plc in October 1998 and until May 1999, she was Marketing Director of the South African Division where she was responsible for marketing and communications.

### Background

Interactive Investor was launched in 1995 to provide online personal finance information to UK consumers. The brand was primarily web based at launch, providing pertinent financial information online.

Interactive Investor Trading Limited, a subsidiary of interactive investor international plc, was granted regulatory status by the SFA in October 1999. From this date the company began to introduce new services allowing consumers to buy and sell selected financial products online.

Following a successful floatation in February 2000 on the London Stock Exchange and Nasdaq, the company sought strategic alliances with a number of leading businesses, providing jointly branded services. Interactive Investor is now adopting a multi-channel approach, providing WAP and digital TV services, in addition to its PC based web service.

### Product/Service

Interactive Investor allows consumers to identify, compare, monitor and buy online a diverse range of financial products and services, ranging from unit trusts and ISAs to insurance, credit cards and pensions.

During 2000 Interactive Investor launched a new ISA centre (ISANow!); a new funds supermarket (FundsNow!) providing access to over 400 funds from 29 UK fund managers; an IPO centre, which was used to manage elements of the online retail offerings of Stepstone and lastminute.com; and a new enhanced equity subscription product providing advanced charting and data facilities – allowing account holders to track the performance of their share portfolio.

Interactive Investor plans to launch an online brokerage facility. The company has also announced a partnership with Towry Law, a firm of Independent Financial Advisers, in order to assist investors making financial decisions. As a consequence, Interactive Investor's users will be able to call a dedicated call centre to receive investment advice at a discounted rate on financial products.

### Promotion

Interactive Investor's marketing and campaign management is key to the success of its business. Using a variety

of media, including targeted press and poster advertising, electronic marketing and direct mail, Interactive Investor aims to attract new users and encourage existing registered account holders to transact online. It has also used innovative marketing methods to help maximise brand awareness such as advertising in phone booths in the Square Mile and a series of interactive road shows across the UK where users can meet the company's senior executives.

Throughout 2000, Interactive Investor ran four advertising campaigns, promoting the major product lines of the business, including the launch of its new funds service, FundsNow! – covering 29 UK fund managers and over 400 funds.

It also began to personalise its email and alerts service, a programme designed to activate its user base and so drive yield for advertisers and product providers.

### Brand Values

Interactive Investor was formed to empower individuals to take control of their finances. It aims to ensure that financial power is in the hands of the consumer by demystifying and simplifying the process of purchasing financial products. It allows consumers to identify, compare, monitor and buy online an extensive range of financial products and services. By doing so, it aims to be the one stop shop for financial shopping online. Interactive Investor's recognisable fluid blue logo, together with the company name, reinforces the company's brand values. Offering different access channels including the web, WAP phone and interactive digital TV, Interactive Investor aims to make financial information easy to understand, impartial and interesting.

### Future Plans

Interactive Investor plans to build on its multi-channel approach, adding to its mobile and TV channels. The company recently announced a digital television service with leading digital company NTL:, and its WAP service has been voted best financial service by Virgin Mobile.

Interactive Investor also intends to encourage more of its substantial user base to transact online. To help achieve this aim, it has restructured its website allowing easier access to core investment product information and decision making support. This support will be provided online and, where appropriate, via telephone and face-to-face meetings. It also plans to launch an online broking facility during 2001, providing straight through processing on equities and funds.

**www.iii.co.uk**

## Market Context

More than one in ten British adults, which equates to 5.1 million people have home access to online gaming and 11% of internet users play games online (Source: Mintel 2000). The UK online games market is the biggest in Europe. In December 2000 there were 2,468,000 visitors to UK game sites (Source: Netvalue) compared with 1,840,000 to games sites in Germany, the UK's closest European competitor.

Operators in this market often target certain types of players. At one end of the spectrum is counterstrike.net which appeals to the more hard core gamer and at the other Tombola and bananalotto, which require little or no skill from the user but offer high value prizes. Jamba falls between these extremes. There are prizes to be won every month and while the games are not complicated, they involve a level of skill rather than luck. The breadth of games – from arcade games to trivia – is designed to appeal to a very broad range of players and gives everyone who participates a chance to win. Jamba encourages an element of competition through the use of high score tables, yet the prizes on offer are not for the top scorer as such. To maintain the sense of achievability the games are given high score hurdle rates. Anybody who scores above the hurdle is automatically entered into a prize draw.

## Achievements

Jamba has over 150,000 unique users per month and has won a number of awards, including the Best Entertainment website in the 1998 Baftas and the Best Entertainment website in the 1999 UK Yell Awards. It was also nominated for the New Media Age Best Entertainment Website in 1999. Following usability studies Jamba has recently gone through a redesign to expose the content more effectively and to add new games to the portfolio. Traffic has increased by 170% following this move.

## Key Management

Duncan Eaton, Marketing and Strategy Director was previously Marketing Director of the Independent. Eaton oversaw the move from separate Carlton internet properties into the umbrella site of Carlton.com in October 2000 following comprehensive commissioned research that suggested that the target market preferred all their entertainment needs in one location. Since the move to Carlton.com total traffic for the company has risen 33%.

## Background

Jamba was developed by Carlton Interactive in November 1998 to exploit the gaming opportunities afforded by the internet. Carlton Interactive is the internet subsidiary of the Carlton

Media Group, owner of the ITV franchise for the South East, Central and West Country and HTV.

### Product/Service

Jamba is targeted at 18-34 year olds. Players can access Jamba through the internet, NTL, Telewest and ONdigital, and also syndicates content for the major portals including MSN, Freeserve and BT.

Jamba concentrates on the fun of the game with the additional bonus of being able to win prizes. Games are low risk, in that players can not lose money, but, with their high score tables, there is a sense of competitiveness.

Gaming on Jamba is free, whereas other gaming sites often use 'pay to play' mechanics, subscription gaming and episodic gaming.

The business model for Jamba was built around traditional banner advertising revenue, but has subsequently been expanded with new innovative trivia games to include in-game interstitial advertising, sponsorship and e-commerce.

It is a site for people who enjoy playing games and winning prizes. It features a wide range of games based around popular TV shows, trivia, classic arcade, card and board games. There are over twenty games that are constantly updated to maintain interest in the site and encourage users to make repeat visits to the site.

### Promotion

Jamba has been advertised on television and radio and is promoted regularly online using banner ads. The most recent range of radio

ads featured Dom Jolly from 'Trigger Happy TV' asking people on the street trivia questions – the most popular area of the site. Another radio campaign highlighted new games to the site, including All Shook Up and Quizino.

All Shook Up was designed to work across all platforms with an interactive game show host asking music trivia from the 1970s, 1980s and 1990s. This has been designed to provide revenue streams through interstitials and sponsorship which creates further revenue streams across interactive TV.

Quizino is a ground-breaking game mixing the thrill of the casino with trivia questions. Using the chips provided users gamble on their ability to answer questions. No money exchanges but there are great prizes to win at each level and again the opportunity for revenue streams in sponsorship and interstitials.

Jamba uses prizes such as holidays or top-of-the-range laptop computers to incentivise play and a weekly email newsletter goes out to over 300,000 people every week to drive traffic back to the site.

### Brand Values

Jamba stands for fun whist being challenging and exciting without high commitment in terms of time or learning. It is a site for people with time to kill but not to waste. It is rewarding in that users are offered chances to win prizes in return for playing.

### Future Plans

The latest edition to the Jamba portfolio is the online version of the ever popular TV quiz show 'Bulls Eye'. Mixing darts with trivia and featuring 'Bully' himself, the game launched in May 2001.

**www.jamba.co.uk**

# JAVA™

## Market Context

The power of the internet lies in its ability to let computers speak to one another, creating a global network of infinite communication. Java is the programming language that allows computers and other networked devices to have this 'dialogue' and, thereby, is one of the technologies that fuels the web. It puts the 'world' into the world wide web.

Due to the limitless scale of the web, it is almost impossible to draw a boundary line around Java's market. It is a technology whose scope is limitless, as it is an open, standard, universal platform for network computing that scales from the simplest consumer devices to mission-critical applications.

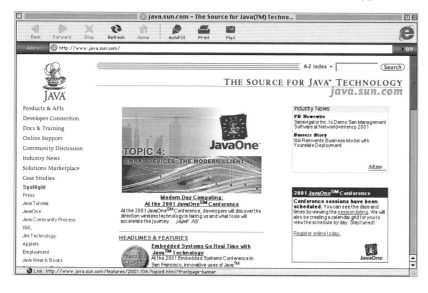

## Achievements

Java is the first ever universal software platform and the technology that accelerated the internet revolution. When it was launched, in 1995, it was a fundamentally new way of computing, based on the concept that the same software should run on many different kinds of computers and digital devices.

This simple but ground-breaking premise led to Java becoming the key enabling technology of all network-centric applications, and it is now used in everything from smart cards to supercomputers.

The invention of Java was like the discovery of a new construction material – like a new kind of steel or concrete – which has allowed the internet to be 'built' faster.

The achievement of Java is part of a bigger picture – the vision of its parent company, Sun Microsystems. Sun's emphasis on developing open architecture – and the creation of Java as the ultimate expression of that vision – showed that, even in the earliest days of the internet, Sun recognised that networking could change global communications.

## Key Management

James Gosling is the Founder of Java and helped create it in the early 1990s. He was appointed as a Fellow of Sun Microsystems in 1996 and is the lead engineer and key architect behind the revolutionary Java programming language.

Gosling has been involved in distributed computing since his arrival at Sun in 1984. His first project was the NeWS window system. Before joining Sun, he built a multiprocessor version of UNIX; the original Andrew window system and toolkit; and several compilers and mail systems. He also built the original UNIX 'Emacs', and helped build a satellite data acquisition system.

Scott McNealy co-founded Sun Microsystems in 1982. In just eighteen years, the company has become the leading global supplier of network computing solutions, with revenues of more than US$14 billion. Since taking the reins as CEO in 1984, McNealy has steered Sun to constant growth and profitability. His vision and business acumen have made him one of the most influential and widely quoted leaders in the complex, fluid, and fast-moving IT industry.

Bill Joy is the Chief Scientist and a Corporate Executive Officer of Sun Microsystems. Bill co-founded Sun in 1982 and was appointed Chief Scientist in 1998. His current research is into new uses of distributed computing enabled using the Java and Jini technologies. He is also involved in new methods of human-computer interaction, new microprocessor and system design.

Bill is the co-recipient, along with Andy Bechtolsheim (also a co-founder of Sun) of the Computerworld Smithsonian award for Innovation in 1999. Bill is a member of the National Academy of Engineering and a fellow of the American Academy of Arts and Sciences.

## Background

To understand the creation of Java, it is necessary to appreciate the philosophy of Sun Microsystems, the company that created it. Its founding vision – 'The Network is the Computer' – showed that it understood very early on that the future was going to be about computers talking to each other, not acting in isolation. While its competitors focused on developing proprietary systems, Sun concentrated on open architecture, and, in 1995, launched Java as a language for the networking future.

The software quickly proved its influence, and was immediately popular. People adopted Java technology for its unique ability to enable the building and deploying of applications that run across any network and on any operating system.

In 1996, Java was licensed to all major hardware and software manufacturers. In 1997, NASA used Java to allow internet users all over the world see pictures of its ground-breaking mission to Mars.

### Product/Service

Java is effectively a language for the internet that allows different computers – of whatever kind – to talk to each other. The Java platform-independent programming product is a write-once, read-anywhere language, able to bring together different technologies and make them work together securely and quickly.

With Java technology, people can use the same application from any kind of machine – a PC, a Macintosh computer, a networked computer or a personal digital assistant like a Palm. Java is incorporated into all major web browsers, allowing people to view web pages. The software's applications can be seen in many forms – for example, the 'applets' which allow interactive functions within web browsers are based on Java.

Java can run on the servers of large companies, monitoring transactions and tying together data from existing computer systems. Companies can also use Java on their internal websites, to streamline the flow of information between departments, suppliers and customers.

Nowadays, Java is used in all sorts of applications, ranging from the simple creation of a web page to complex tasks like building automation systems for the automotive and aerospace industries.

The Java product line is extensive, with the Java 2 Platform being the starting point. This provides a comprehensive, end-to-end architecture for building and deploying network-centric applications for the enterprise and consumer. The Java 2 Enterprise Edition (J2EE) is an enhanced version, designed for businesses. Another variation is Java 2 Platform Micro Edition,

which is designed for consumer products like pagers, mobile phones and digital set-top boxes.

### Promotion

Sun generates publicity for Java from high-profile industry conventions, such as the annual JESS (Java Enterprise Solutions Symposium). This is where the latest technological innovations and discussions about the e-economy take place – attracting significant media interest and valuable column inches.

Sun also uses specially produced magazines to highlight its strength in different areas, such as '.Com in Sport' and '.Com Your Business'. It also published handy internet pocket guides, such as the '.Com Guide to Life'. These provide a practical insight into Sun's wide range of products, including Java. On top of this printed material, Sun uses its website, www.sun.com, to promote its wide range of services and products.

### Brand Values

The founding slogan of Java is 'write once, run anywhere'. This encapsulates the idea that one piece of software can be used across multiple operating systems on multiple devices, helping them all to interconnect and communicate. With this in mind, Java's other core values include sharing, enablement, empowerment and simplicity. Java is also about making people's and company's – lives better by making things work better together.

Java's brand values are closely linked to those of Sun, whose pioneering faith in open architecture informs its core belief that 'The Network is the Computer.'

### Future Plans

As the web matures and develops in new directions, so does the reach of Java. For example, as the mobile internet takes off, the Java platform is expanding into the wireless environment and, as the line between TV and the internet blurs, Java is moving into that area too, incorporating its technology into set-top boxes. In the future, the internet will be accessible by a much wider range of consumer devices – perhaps even household appliances like a fridge – and Java will have a role to play in making these devices interconnect.

**www.java.sun.com**

# lastminute.com

## Market Context

In a volatile market, B2C startups have come and gone, bricks and mortar companies have realised the opportunities (and challenges) that e-commerce brings and media scrutiny has been intense – in this context lastminute.com has not only survived, but thrived. Since its inception and subsequent acquisition of leading French e-commerce company Degriftour in October 2000 it has helped over one million customers 'do something lastminute.com'.

## Achievements

Since the first transaction was made on the website in October 1998, lastminute.com has grown at an astonishing rate. The freshness of the idea meant that the company became a by-word for the excitement that accompanied the proliferation of internet startups in 1998 and 1999, gaining new suppliers, new subscribers and new customers at an exponential rate – with a corresponding growth in staff. lastminute.com floated on the London Stock Exchange in March 2000, raising a significant amount of capital to fund the long-term growth of the company.

Perhaps more impressive has been the company's achievements since the Initial Public Offering, in a market where investors and the media have

and entrepreneurial spirit of a startup while developing a trusted brand and established processes to plan and manage growth.

## Key Management

Brent Hoberman, Co Founder and CEO, set up lastminute.com with Martha Lane Fox in April 1998 and the site was launched to the public in October that year. Before setting up lastminute.com, Hoberman was General Manager, Head of Business Development and a founding member of QXL, a leading online auction business. Prior to this he worked in business development at one of the UK's first internet service providers, LineOne and spent five years in strategy consulting, specialising in the media and telecoms, first at Mars & Co and then at Spectrum Strategy Consultants as a Senior Associate. Brent holds an MA from Oxford University.

Martha Lane Fox, Co Founder and Group Managing Director, was formerly Head of Network Development at Carlton Digital Channels where she was responsible for generating and analysing new channel and interactive concepts. Her responsibilities included negotiating with UK and international distribution partners to develop the Carlton brand overseas. Prior to Carlton, Martha worked for three years as an Associate at Spectrum Strategy Consultants where she specialized in 'pay television' and managed teams in both the UK and Asia. She holds an MA from Oxford University.

## Background

Brent Hoberman and Martha Lane Fox founded lastminute.com in Hoberman's living room in April 1998, having both abandoned secure jobs, to build an e-commerce company from nothing. The website launched in October of that year, and in only two years has become one of the best-known e-commerce brands in Europe – a publicly-quoted company with live sites in nine countries and the epitome of a dotcom start up in the public mind.

lastminute.com was based on the simple idea of using the internet to match last minute supply with last minute demand, both for inspiration and convenience. For suppliers, lastminute.com can provide an online distribution channel for last minute inventory that would otherwise go

become increasingly sceptical about the future prospects of some dotcom companies, lastminute.com has continued to meet and exceed analysts' expectations and to delight customers in this environment. lastminute.com retains the rapid growth

unsold. Suppliers ranging from some of the largest national airline carriers to the smallest independent hotels can sell their products to a huge national and international customer base. Suppliers can benefit from lastminute.com's technology platforms and the strength of the lastminute.com brand. This business model means that lastminute.com takes minimal inventory risk.

For customers, lastminute.com provides a convenient one-stop place for all kinds of last minute transactions. As well as potentially being the first place to look for specific products or services, lastminute.com also aims to offer inspiration to users by aggregating lots of different suppliers and products into one place. It provides everything from flowers to the chance to drive a Ferrari, a table at one of London's top restaurants to a secluded country hotel, a city break to Paris or even the trip of a lifetime to the Maldives.

## Product/Service
lastminute.com aims to be the first place to look for inspiration and solutions at the last minute. Currently the product range on offer is broken down into five top line categories – travel (flights, hotel rooms and package holidays), going out (restaurant bookings and tickets to events of all kinds), experiences (everything from bungee jumps to spa days), sports (tickets, specialist holidays and hospitality) and shopping (including an auctions function).

## Promotion
To establish a position as one of Britain's most recognized e-commerce brands and most visited e-commerce multi-category websites, lastminute.com has employed all elements of the marketing mix. A high-visibility offline marketing campaign concentrated on a well-defined target audience helped establish the brand without the high costs associated with TV advertising, while a wide-ranging online distribution strategy helps deliver traffic and revenues to the site in a cost-effective way.

lastminute.com now has over 3.1 million subscribers who receive the famous weekly email newsletter – a unique mix of special offers and topical content delivered to their inboxes, establishing a regular and ongoing relationship between the site and its customers. A pioneering use of viral marketing online has helped generate traffic and 'talkability' at a very low cost, with innovative projects like the unbranded Office Flirt Test attracting hundreds of thousands of users to the site, passed virally to friends and colleagues around the globe.

## Brand Values
The lastminute.com brand is about providing inspirational solutions for every occasion. This is fundamental to the ethos of the company and goes beyond just marketing or advertising – as demonstrated by the company's mission statement: 'lastminute.com wants to encourage spontaneous, romantic and sometimes adventurous behaviour by offering people the chance to live their dreams at unbeatable prices.'

## Future Plans
As well as being available on the web, the lastminute.com service can be accessed via WAP enabled mobile phones, interactive digital TV and handheld devices such as Palm Pilots or Psion organisers. Over Christmas 2000, the company also launched a prototype of what it believes to be the world's first fully-transactional voice recognition multi-category commerce service, allowing customers to buy products from any phone, effectively 'talking' to the product database. lastminute.com will continue to invest in new and as yet unknown digital platforms as they emerge.

**www.lastminute.com**

# MAPQUEST

## Market Context

Online mapping has become a popular sector on the internet, as people increasingly use the web for practical purposes like finding directions for places to which they are travelling or sending maps to friends and colleagues. Businesses also use online mapping to drive brand impact, improve customer satisfaction and increase revenue by promoting store locations on interactive maps and providing door-to-door driving directions to their store locations for their website users.

As such, online mapping is a sector that straddles the B2B and B2C markets. As e-commerce has grown to become a US$100 billion market, MapQuest is in a strong position to help businesses provide one-click answers to customers' most frequently asked questions and provide consumers with useful localised content that is necessary for everyday activities. While the growth in PC-based e-commerce is important to MapQuest, the brand is also poised to benefit from the growing area of mobile ebusiness. Wireless internet access will create even greater demand for online location information, as people will be able to find directions to places when they are on the go. This mobile information market is expected to be worth $20 billion by 2005 (Source: Mobile Lifestreams).

## Achievements

MapQuest.com is ranked the 28th most powerful website worldwide (Source: MMXI March 2001), with every one in five internet users accessing its content each month and more than twenty million MapQuest maps downloaded every day.

Not all of these maps are drawn from the MapQuest.com or MapQuest.co.uk websites. MapQuest licenses its business solutions to two thousand business partners and there are more than 300,000 links to MapQuest information from other web pages.

MapQuest has a rare quality in the new media space – a reputation that stretches back many years. It has been a pioneer in mapping since the 1960s and now provides more highly detailed, global map coverage than any other online cartographic or internet mapping company.

Its pioneering achievements include: in 1994, the first interactive mapping product for the world's first handheld computer – the Apple Newton MessagePad. In 1996, the MapQuest.com website was the first consumer-focused online mapping service.

Also, MapQuest's Travel Guide and directions services for web-enabled mobile phone users have been successful. Available on BT's GenieMobile, the service allows users to find directions to restaurants, hotels and other venues, or turn by turn route-finding directions for locations all over the UK. This product was one of the first location-based services available for wireless mobile internet users and its popularity is a testament to its usefulness. Within six months of launch, in January 2000, there were more than one million requests for MapQuest data from the GenieMobile service. In addition, the product was runner up in the Personal Information Product category at the IM2000 Information Management Awards.

## Key Management

Todd Walrath is Chief Operating Officer of MapQuest responsible for managing all business areas of the company, Todd oversees the management team in the US and worldwide. He joined the company from Weather.com, which he helped grow from six employees to 192.

Michael Nappi was one of MapQuest's founding executives, leading its growth and success by developing internet distribution models and B2B partnerships. He helped grow the business from three to 150 employees and grow revenue by more than 1000%. He is now in a broader role with MapQuest's parent company, America Online, overseeing the implementation of AOL's Local Business Solutions for B2B marketing.

Ed Mance is Vice President, International Business Development, and as such, is responsible for the global expansion of MapQuest. Ed has a seventeen year background in the development of new markets and alliances within new media.

## Background

MapQuest dates back to the 1960s, when it was founded by RR Donnelley & Sons in Pennsylvania. It was originally set up as cartographic services division to create road maps, which were then given to petrol station customers for free. By the 1970s, MapQuest was a leading supplier of custom maps to reference, travel, textbook and directory publishers. Soon, it had a reputation as a high-quality custom mapmaker working for clients such as American Express, National Geographic and Readers Digest.

In 1991, MapQuest pioneered electronic publishing software for

## Let Us Show You the Way

interactive mapping applications and during the early 1990s, earned a reputation for providing electronic mapping services for call centres, kiosks, client-server environments and award-winning CD-ROMs for travel, directory and road atlas mapping products. In 1994, its product for the handheld Apple Newton opened up a new market for 'travel cartridges' containing city guides, driving and walking tours and directory mapping. These cartridges were used by brands such as Fodors, Michelin and TimeOut.

In 1996, MapQuest launched the first-ever consumer-focused interactive mapping site on the web and a B2B service to map-enable other websites.

In June 2000, MapQuest.com was acquired by America Online, Inc and the company is now a wholly owned subsidiary of AOL.

In February 2001, the company launched its web service in the UK, extending its geocentric information services for twelve European countries and in nine languages.

Together with the UK consumer site, MapQuest Direct was launched to provide a free online mapmaking service for small to medium-sized websites that allows for fast and easy integration of mapping and driving directions.

### Product/Service

MapQuest.com and MapQuest.co.uk are free online mapping services. As well as generating maps, according to the user's specified request, the sites also provide driving directions that yield the most direct route from a point of origin to a destination in a variety of ways, such as text-only, overview

map with text, or turn by turn directions. Travel information is another important product area, providing access to lodging, dining and other city information, such as scenic drives and walks.

MapQuest's extensive database provides geocentric information with maps for every country in the world and extensive street-level mapping for most major international tourist and business destinations. The online maps are easy to print, download and email.

MapQuest's service is also available to users of wireless devices for people on the go. The MapQuest Travel Guide

provides a searchable directory of nearby useful venues such as hotels, restaurants and retailers with turn by turn directions. The service is available on WAP mobile phones and handheld devices through AOL Mobile, Genie Mobile and Palm Computing.

MapQuest also provides extensive B2B services. MapQuest's business solutions enable other websites to provide location-finding maps for their customers. In the UK, a new service, called MapQuest Direct, allows businesses to build maps for their websites with a free and easy-to-use, online mapmaking tool for small to medium-sized businesses.

### Promotion

MapQuest advertises to consumers and businesses. To attract the B2B audience, its advertisements can be found in the trade press including M-Commerce World and Information Age. It also exhibits and advertises at trade shows and exhibitions. To grab consumers' attention, it employs a variety of location-centric techniques, including the use of postcard-sized 'Go-Cards' which were distributed in bars and restaurants throughout London for the launch of MapQuest.co.uk. The value and convenience of online mapping and local content provides MapQuest with the ability to build a loyal following through C2C referrals.

### Brand Values

MapQuest is the internet's most popular source for maps and driving directions. Its extensive cartographic coverage of the globe is available in a wide range of user-friendly formats. MapQuest strives to provide the best information in formats that consumers and businesses find easy to use. In addition to pioneering online mapping on the web, MapQuest has pushed into the wireless arena, providing its services via WAP phones and personal digital assistants (PDAs). Being a pioneer and 'pushing the envelope' of technology to provide useful solutions for consumers and businesses are at the heart of the brand.

### Future Plans

As a premiere location-based solutions provider, MapQuest's mission is to be an invaluable part of people's everyday lives, providing travellers and customers with the tools to access mapping and driving directions anytime, anywhere. Key areas of development for MapQuest will be in continuing to broaden its already extensive global reach, providing increasing coverage at an even more detailed level for the whole world. Extending the company's influence in the wireless space will also be a priority, especially as G3 broadband devices begin to come onto the market over the next five years. The wireless internet is set to explode and MapQuest is in a prime position to raise its profile even further.

**www.mapquest.co.uk**

# marbles™
## www.marbles.com

### Market Context

There are well over 1,000 different credit cards in the UK offering an extensive range of interest rates and features. Annual spend on our 'flexible friends' is £82 billion (Source: British Bankers Association 1999) and notably increasing year-on-year. Coupled with this, is the rapid advance of e-commerce and consumers' willingness to purchase goods via their credit cards over the internet. Figures estimate that online shopping in the UK grew from £0.9 billion in 1999 to £2.4 billion in 2000 (Source: Jupiter Research 2000). However, not everyone is happy at the prospect of tapping their credit card number into a computer, sending it off into the ether and then crossing their fingers and hoping the goods arrive.

HFC Bank is the UK's fifth largest credit card issuer with over 2.5 million cards in circulation. Its marbles™ brand and credit card product recognises the impact of e-commerce and the need to demystify the internet in a simple and non-threatening way to consumers.

### Achievements

Since its launch in October 1999 marbles™ has firmly established its internet and credit card credentials. A card base of over 200,000 has been rapidly built and the innovative brand has achieved exceptionally high levels of awareness (Source: HPI Research). Furthermore, amid some high profile financial internet launches and subsequent crashes, marbles™ continued to provide a reliable 24 hour service seven days a week.

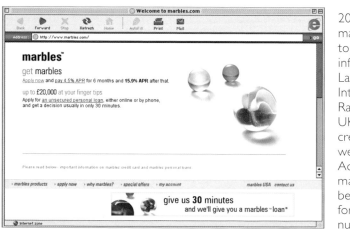

September 2000, saw marbles™ topping the influential Lafferty Internet Ratings of UK online credit card websites. Additionally, marbles™ has been put forward for numerous

awards in the marketing and technology innovation fields. Notably, given the emphasis placed on brand language, it won the 'Best Use of Copy' category at the Campaign Direct Awards 2000.

marbles™ is now a serious player in the credit card market and a leader in internet friendly credit cards. It is seen as a modern, pioneering brand with a good internet-based infrastructure and sufficient brand stretch to move into other financial product areas.

The marbles™ brand has already extended its reach to the US where HFC Bank's parent company Household International is marketing a marbles™ retail point of sale product.

marbles™ was not just about a new credit card. The launch called for HFC Bank to internet-enable its business both in terms of its IT infrastructure, business processes and staff skill sets.

### Key Management

Concept to launch took just four short months and the HFC Bank team was led by Group Marketing Director, Mark Robinson, closely supported by Marketing Director, Jane Perrins who drove the integrated communications programme, e-Commerce Director, Ian Coles who spearheaded the deployment of the brand over the internet and Director of Corporate Affairs, Martin Rutland who handled public relations.

Robinson, who has over eleven years of financial services experience, co-ordinated a multi-disciplined marketing effort that called on the resources of experts in their respective fields, notably Wolff Olins (brand design), Mother (advertising) and Clark McKay and Walpole (direct marketing).

### Background

During 1999 there was a rapid explosion of internet usage fuelled by free ISPs and a corresponding increase in the amount of goods and services being bought over the internet. HFC Bank's strategy has been, in simple terms, to help people organise their credit and to be there when people wanted to buy things. Therefore, HFC Bank needed a way to move its lending products online. The Bank was in the fortunate position of having

some people would rather sell their own grandma than use their credit card online. other people are **protected from fraud by marbles**, so they can go on the internet and buy someone else's grandma without worrying.

now you can pay with **marbles**

www.getmarbles.co.uk or call 0845 600 63 36

got ahead and completed its Y2K systems work and its Chief Executive, Adrian Hill saw a window of opportunity while some rivals focused on beating the 'Millennium Bug'. Two things were needed – a brand that could stand for 'money on the net' and a truly internet-enabled credit card. HFC Bank also identified that while the internet offered a whole new way to buy things there was a reluctance for many people in the mass market to take the plunge or run their credit card online.

marbles™ addressed this considerable opportunity when the marbles™ credit card was launched in October 1999.

## Product/Service

marbles™ is a no fee, competitively priced credit card that can be applied for online with an answer received within 60 seconds. Additionally, a marbles™ customer can choose to run an account entirely online, making payments, looking up old statements and seeing what transactions are pending. Importantly, because it is recognised that not everyone is comfortable with using the internet, the card can be applied for by post or telephone and all customers receive a normal monthly statement. Also, because customers are not always happy dealing online, a 24-hour customer service line is also provided.

marbles™ research had shown that potential customers' major concerns were about security of making purchases over the internet and the sheer size, complexity and jargon associated with the world of e-commerce. In response the marbles™ credit card offers a safe shopping promise that says if anyone else uses the customer's credit number over the internet they don't have to pay. It also uses a language which talks to people in a playful, matter of fact and non-technical way.

## Promotion

It was essential, due to the short lead time, that an environment was created where the strategy was mutually developed rather than the traditional, staid and time consuming formal client brief.

An integrated marketing campaign was employed to establish the marbles™ brand and to recruit over 200,000 cardholders. This used a variety of media, with high profile national television advertising, selected online presence and PR activity quickly building brand awareness followed by carefully targeted direct mail to creditworthy households.

In order to further establish the card's credentials and generate an additional channel for customer recruitment, a co-branded card was launched with Freeserve, one of the UK's leading ISPs.

Since launch a number of other co-branded marbles™ cards have been launched with partners such as QXL and Internet Exchange.

## Brand Values

The original brief was to develop a brand that could stand for 'Money on the Net'. However, the brand needed to have a personality that was modern, human and playful. This would enable marbles™ to differentiate itself from the cold, impersonal and traditional finance brands. A brand language was developed which talked to people in a human and playful way. For example, the online application process was introduced with the words, 'this will take a few minutes so why not go and make yourself a cup of tea' rather than 'this file is now downloading'.

## Future Plans

Given the speed with which the internet is developing, marbles™ is striving to continue to be a brand that evolves and keeps ahead of customer trends. For example, whilst still very relevant, strong security credentials alone are no longer a differentiator as this type of offering has become a hygiene factor in the credit card market and people are becoming increasingly comfortable with shopping over the net. The next challenge is to develop a relationship with customers that they truly value as they feel they are being kept one step ahead in this fast moving new world.

marbles™ aims to be much more than just a credit card. It is HFC Bank's way of becoming as good at providing credit products online as it is in the offline world today. marbles™ direct loans has already been launched along with marbles™ e-tail finance, where marbles™ loans are offered via retailers' own websites (another industry first).

Finally, following the successful launch, the marbles™ model will be used within HFC Bank to test out creative ways of working with multi-agency teams.

**www.marbles.com**

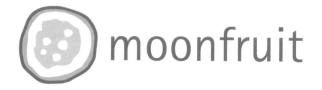

# moonfruit

## Market Context

Core to Moonfruit's strategy is the recognition that it is people who use the internet. Many have little time and limited patience for what is often a dry and complicated internet environment. They will keep looking around until they find a site that answers their needs. Online portals are all fighting to 'own the user' but the user refuses to be owned. People will become loyal users of a service on their own terms: and that means that those services must offer an interactive, personalised environment.

Moonfruit is a developer of multimedia applications, designed to help online businesses provide a personalised, richly interactive user experience. Moonfruit's first application enables people to build their own Flash-based, highly personalised websites in a 'live' online environment. Whether you want to put your sports club online, express your devotion for Tiger Woods or create an electronic CV, Moonfruit's application enables anyone to achieve a highly professional online presence and have fun whilst doing so.

There are many other players in this market offering website building tools on the internet, and many more who have declared their aim to help businesses retain and monetise their user base. Moonfruit claims that its offering is different because it doesn't look for conventional solutions. Both entertaining and useful, Moonfruit's application helps its clients achieve their core objectives: winning more users, building loyalty and generating new revenue streams.

## Achievements

Founded in August 1999, Moonfruit set out to give people the tools to make their internet experience enriching, entertaining and user-friendly. Moonfruit.com, the consumer website-building portal, was developed in just four months and launched in the UK in January 2000. It was the world's first Flash-based website-building

application. More than 60,000 websites were built using Moonfruit.com in the first year.

The first release of Moonfruit.com was highly acclaimed, with several awards nominations culminating in winning BBC2's Online Design Award 2000. The second release was launched in November 2000.

## Key Management

Wendy Tan, CEO, founded Moonfruit in the summer of 1999. Wendy studied Computer Science at Imperial College, London, and then Management Science at Cranfield. She began her career as a consultant

for Arthur Andersen, before becoming Business Consultancy Manager at AIT plc, a software development business. More recently Wendy joined Egg to set up the marketing department, and then became E-partnerships manager, negotiating deals with AOL, Excite and Yahoo!.

Will Gardner, former Marketing Director, joined Moonfruit in December 1999 from brand consultants The Added Value Company. After graduating with a degree in English from Trinity College, Cambridge, Will joined Mars in 1992 as a graduate trainee. He held various marketing roles in Mars in the UK and internationally, ending up managing new product launches, branding and communications for three Mars pet food brands across Europe.

## Background

Moonfruit went live in January 2000 with the launch of its consumer website-building portal, Moonfruit.com.

In March 2000 Moonfruit.com was named Macromedia's Site of the Day, increasing awareness on both sides of the Atlantic. In April the consumer marketing campaign began: a combination of television, press and online advertising. Named Revolution magazine's Campaign of the Week, at its peak it inspired more than 700 people daily to build personal websites.

Moonfruit.com was already proving the popularity of the website-building tool, and it wasn't long before other consumer portals began to approach Moonfruit, asking whether it was possible to license the Moonfruit technology as a service for their

users. To respond to this demand, Moonfruit began to develop a new, licensable version of its software.

In July 2000 Moonfruit formalised its positioning as a developer and provider of interactive multimedia applications. Moonfruit is now selling its website-building toolkit as a customised application to media companies and portals.

### Product/Service

Moonfruit is committed to enriching and simplifying the internet experience via multiple devices. As a developer of interactive applications, Moonfruit aims to be in a position to reach millions of users worldwide via a network of local and global clients.

Moonfruit has developed a Flash-based infrastructure and a versatile library of multimedia features and content. Moonfruit is able to assemble these features and this content into different applications which meet a range of client and end user needs.

The first of these applications is the website-building tool, which enables people to express themselves and share their interests online. For example, a member of a sports club is able to build a website, into which he can drop pre-configured features (a photo gallery, a directory of club members and a club news section) along with photographs, music and customised news feeds.

The website-building tool is licensed to media companies and portals as a hosted application, customised (in terms of branding and content) to meet the client's specific needs. Clients in turn provide the website-building toolkit as a cutting-edge service to their users, who (as site owners) become much more active, loyal customers.

### Promotion

Moonfruit has so far promoted its website-building toolkit to both users and to potential licensing clients.

PR has played a major role in the development of the Moonfruit brand. The launch of Moonfruit.com was celebrated by a three-page feature in The Guardian's online section; and since then Moonfruit has benefited from

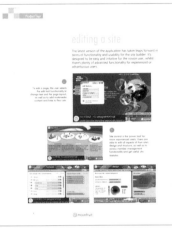

substantial coverage in national broadsheets, 'Site of the Month' accolades in trade publications and features in consumer titles.

For Moonfruit, planning the consumer marketing campaign in early 2000 proved to be a considerable challenge. Its aim was to build awareness of the brand name and the service offering as fast as possible, in an expensive media environment overwhelmed by 'dotcom clutter'. However, in the UK personal website building was still in its infancy. This meant that Moonfruit had to answer the question 'why should I build a website?' Creating the market was more important than communicating the brand's competitive edge.

Consistent with the brand's quirky essence, Moonfruit decided to portray groups of people sharing their interests, but always with an unusual twist: for example, robotics dancers at a coffee morning, bishops swapping football cards, naked artists 'bumpainting'. The message was: 'Share your passion – build your own free website with Moonfruit.com.'

To drive interest and awareness, the campaign began on TV in high internet-using regions of the UK, supported by an online campaign on major UK portals. Then Moonfruit used press advertising in the specialist press (internet, sport, music and film) to reinforce the call to action.

Capitalising on the benefits of high industry awareness, Moonfruit has since recently concentrated its marketing efforts on supporting the licensing of the website-building tool to online portals and media companies. Focusing on a small number of target clients, Moonfruit has produced marketing collateral in-house, and has otherwise been focusing on PR coverage and trade exhibitions.

### Brand Values

The Moonfruit brand is an incarnation of the Moonfruit staff's passion for making the internet enriching, fun and user friendly.

Moonfruit promises the user that they will be empowered to make new, life-enriching connections. Moonfruit's users and clients should always find Moonfruit to be highly innovative and occasionally quirky, but with a near-obsessive commitment to quality and customer service.

### Future Plans

The internet is increasingly a vehicle for multimedia communications and personalised services, through your PC, TV or mobile phone. In this fast-developing world, the Moonfruit brand will become known as an enabler – enriching, simplifying, and personalising these experiences.

Moonfruit is beginning to expand internationally, and already has a commercial presence in Germany, France and the US.

**www.moonfruit.com**

## Market Context

Moreover.com is one of a very few significant players in the relatively new market of online news and information aggregation services. Moreover's unique search technology allows companies to make the best use of the information available on the internet and thus offers unique and powerful business intelligence solutions for companies. While it faces competition from syndicators such as Lexis-Nexis and Screaming Media, no other company focuses singularly on the information held within the dynamic part of the internet. This differentiation means Moreover is the most comprehensive supplier of up-to-the-minute online information from around the web. Also, Moreover's ability to harvest any sort of dynamic information, from newswires to intranets and websites to newsgroups, means that it can reach the parts of the web that other search engines and business intelligence tools cannot.

```
Air Rage Diverts 747; Passenger Subdued - Chicago Tribune    powered by
                                                             moreover ●●●
```

## Achievements

Moreover's talented team of staff, proprietary technology and long term partnerships have established the company's reputation as a next-generation provider of dynamic content and information for websites, search engines and applications.

Moreover has been voted one of The Net magazine's top 50 websites of all time. It was also ranked seventh in The Sunday Times e-league list of

the 100 hottest European dotcom companies, and has won general industry recognition as a leader in web based business intelligence solutions.

Moreover's 'web-feeds' appear on over 65,000 websites, intranets and extranets. As well as the website newsfeeds, many well-known blue chip clients including BT, The Economist and Charles Schwab employ Moreover's powerful business intelligence solutions.

## Key Management

Nick Denton, CEO, co-founded Moreover in 1998 after eight years as a writer with The Economist and Financial Times. He served as the FT's investment banking correspondent during the financial collapses of the mid1990s before arriving in Silicon Valley as the newspaper's US technology correspondent.

Featured in The Guardian e50 list as one of the UK's leading internet entrepreneurs, Nick also played a leading role in founding First Tuesday, a networking organization for the web community that developed into one of Europe's most closely followed start-ups, hosting events in over 80 cities around the world.

He is co-author of All That Glitters, an account of the collapse of Barings bank in 1995. The book was short-listed for the Global Business Book Awards.

Nick remains active in the day to day operations of the company, dividing his time between Moreover's main offices in San Francisco and London.

Angus Bankes, CTO and Co-Founder, graduated in Biotechnology from Kings College London and guides the technical team in their continued development of dynamic information technology. He was co-founder of Match Healthcare Services Inc, a large British health care staffing company that is now part of Sinclair Montrose, the publicly listed company. He is also co-founder, with David Galbraith, of Origins, an internet company that provides access to

the largest genealogy database on the internet. Named by Real Business as one of the top 30 UK internet start-ups, Origins was profitable in its first year.

With David Galbraith, Angus co-developed the MatchNet online staffing system, a sophisticated and highly respected enterprise software system based entirely on internet technologies. His work with Moreover's technology has earned him praise from the press and increasing recognition as a database innovator in the XML community.

David Galbraith, Chief Architect and Co-Founder, leads the product team in San Francisco and continues to pioneer XML-related information technology on the internet. A certified architect, he began his involvement in database technology while working for Foster and Partners, the UK's leading architecture practice. While there, he began designing object-oriented databases for coordination of large-scale construction projects.

David is co-founder, along with Angus Bankes, of the internet genealogy company Origins, and was co-developer of the MatchNet online staffing system. He has worked with internet technologies since 1993 and has been active in the development of XML-related technology since its inception. He was co-author of EDML, a standard for metadata and EDI on the web.

## Background

Moreover was founded in 1998. By designing and engineering dynamic indexing technology, its founders intended to reshape the way information moves on the web. Launched in 1999, Moreover first applied this technology to news, enabling websites to publish fresh, automated headlines in hundreds of categories, collected from thousands of the best sources on the web. The company has since built a far-reaching Dynamic Web Database to reach beyond the news and keep pace with the relentless transformations of the internet.

In June 2000 Moreover received second round funding of $21 million from a distinguished group of backers led by Wit SoundView Ventures and Reuters Venture Capital. Other backers include Advance.net which oversees the internet vision and strategy for Advance Publications Inc, a privately owned media company that owns daily newspapers in 22 cities and national magazines such as Wired, The New Yorker, Vogue, Glamour, and Vanity Fair; Atlas Venture, a transatlantic venture capital firm with $1.6 billion under management; and Richard Tahta, a former Strategic Development Director for Amazon.com in Europe and a co-founder of Chase Episode I, a $100 million UK fund from Chase Capital Partners.

## Product/Service

Moreover's proprietary search and indexing technology continually scans over 2000 selected online sources, harvesting and automatically categorising the headline information. These headlines are delivered to websites and intranets as a 'webfeed', a customised collection of news headlines that update every fifteen minutes to produce the most recent information published online. These dynamic links from thousands of sources can be presented together on a single page, making the internet a unified business intelligence tool.

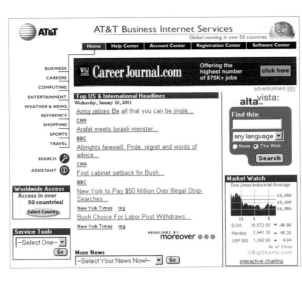

Moreover's technology harvests data from a huge variety of sites – from national newspapers to niche newsgroups. It has a team of qualified editors who evaluate every source gathered to make certain that the database contains only the best and most valuable content found on the internet. Webfeeds consist solely of links to information from robust, editorially sound and professional sites. This ensures that the information clients receive is valuable, timely and relevant.

As part of its brand building activities, Moreover also supplies free newsfeeds to subscriber sites.

## Promotion

Moreover has relied almost entirely on below-the-line marketing and PR activity in the development of the Moreover.com brand. PR has focused on the development of the brand as a forward looking technology company, adding value to websites around the world.

All the free newsfeeds, which sit on subscriber sites, contain Moreover branding which is seen by up to one million users per day.

Moreover has also developed its brand among trade audiences through organising and sponsoring renowned new media networking events.

## Brand Values

Moreover represents a robust technology infrastructure that has become essential to the internet. Through continual innovation and a forward-looking strategy Moreover has earned its reputation as a next-generation provider of dynamic content and information for websites, search engines and applications.

## Future Plans

Moreover plans to use both strategic partnerships and in-house marketing campaigns to increase its presence in the corporate world and to boost its traffic. The company recently announced partnerships with Inktomi, who will offer Moreover's database as part of its search offerings and iWon, the world's fastest growing portal. Moreover has also formed partnerships

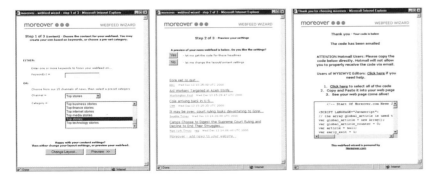

with Microsoft, PeopleSoft and Plumtree. It plans to develop direct relationships with large corporations in order to provide them with internal information solutions.

**www.moreover.com**

## Market Context

Music continues to be one of the most popular forms of entertainment in the world and transcends geographic boundaries and demographic distinctions. Music is also big business. According to the International Federation of the Phonographic Industry, worldwide sales of recorded music were $38.5 billion in 1999. The structure and operation of the music industry has remained relatively unchanged for many years. Artists are generally required to sign exclusive contracts with record labels, which, in turn, develop, distribute and promote their music. In addition, major record labels, as well as a few 'independent' labels, control to a large extent the type and quality of recorded music available to consumers. Due to these limitations, the number of artists served by the traditional music distribution system is small compared to the universe of musicians with commercial aspirations.

MP3.com has pioneered a revolutionary approach to the promotion, distribution, access and management of digital music. The MP3.com website is a premier online music destination with almost one million songs and audio files from about 150,000 digital artists, representing one of the largest catalogues of digital music available on the internet today. The company uses the internet and the widely accepted MP3 compression technology to enable the underserved and growing number of artists to broadly distribute and promote their music and to enable consumers around the world to conveniently access this continually expanding music catalogue. Consumers can search for, listen to and download music free of charge on the MP3.com website.

In addition to the wide variety of music distributed by artists through the MP3.com website, consumers have a substantial amount of music already in their personal music collections that they want to access, manage and listen to in a variety of ways. Just as consumers use an ISP as the central mechanism through which they interact with the internet, individuals are increasingly looking for one central resource that allows them to access, manage and listen to all music. Not just 'new' music, but music already in their personal collections. MP3.com calls this resource a Music Service Provider (MSP). As the premier MSP, MP3.com offers its My.MP3 service which is designed to facilitate the storage, management, promotion and delivery of digital music, and to enable users to listen to their music when they want, where they want by accessing any web-enabled device.

## Achievements

MP3.com's music library has grown from 100,000 songs from 18,000 artists at the time it went public in July 1999 to a catalogue approaching one million songs representing over 150,000 artists in March 2001. The float raised $383 million, making MP3.com one of the largest internet Initial Public Offerings. It enjoys higher revenue growth, more unique visitors, greater and faster growing content and more songs listened to than any of its competitors. In addition, in February 2001, Media Metrix judged it as one of the top five music sites in the US and one of the top five entertainment sites in all of Europe.

In 2000, MP3.com became the only music site to receive North American licenses from all five of the major music labels to include their content in the My.MP3 service. The My.MP3 service allows users to create online music lockers where they can store, organise and manage their favourite songs from music posted by digital artists on the MP3.com website and receive personalised music services. With the introduction of the Beam-it™ and Instant Listening™ features of the My.MP3 service, consumers have the ability to access, add to and manage their existing music CD collections online without having to encode and store tracks themselves. Under this system, once MP3.com is able to determine that a consumer purchased a CD (through the Instant Listening™ feature) or was already in possession of a CD (through the Beam-it™ software), the music from that CD becomes available in the consumer's My.MP3 music locker.

MP3.com has recently opened a European office and has launched French, German, Spanish and Japanese versions of its website to expand its global appeal and better position itself to capitalise on international strategic and revenue-generating opportunities.

## Key Management

Michael L Robertson founded MP3.com and has served as CEO and Chairman since March 1998. From September 1995 Robertson operated several websites that focused on merging search technologies with commerce. Between September 1995 and September 1996 he was president and CEO of Media Minds Inc, a developer of digital picture software and before that was President and CEO of MR Mac Software, a developer of networking and security tools. Other members of the team include:

Robin D Richards has been President and a Director of MP3.com since January 1999.

Paul L H Ouyang has been Chief Financial Officer and Executive Vice President since February 1999.

Derrick R Oien, who joined MP3.com in July 1999, is Senior Vice President and COO.

Steven G Sheiner has served as Executive Vice President, Sales and Marketing since February 1999.

Gregory P Kostello came to MP3.com in June 1999 and serves as Executive Vice President, Technology.

Carolyn J Kantor joined MP3.com in July 1999 and currently serves as President of MP3.com International.

## Background

In 1996 Michael Robertson founded The Z Company, whose primary focus was merging search technologies and commerce. As President, he established Filez, the net's largest and fastest file search engine as well as Websitez, a domain-name search engine and in November 1997, started MP3.com which rapidly became one of the leading music destinations on the internet.

## Product/Service

MP3.com currently operates in B2C as well as B2B segments. The MP3.com music destination website and the My.MP3.com service, which are primarily advertising-supported business models, comprise the B2C offerings. On the MP3.com website, in addition to finding music, consumers can also subscribe to the first ever on-demand internet music subscription channels, send musical greeting cards, learn about MP3 hardware and software, build their own radio station, as well as other music-related activities.

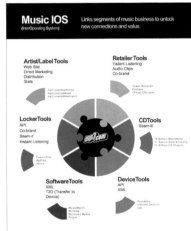

Through its ongoing efforts to develop, maintain and improve the website, MP3.com has amassed a significant amount of expertise in rich media data storage, delivery and management; server-side security; real-time statistical analysis; and royalty tracking and payment systems. Leveraging these core competencies as well as its robust technology infrastructure, MP3.com has developed a number of unique products and services including

innovative business music services, a syndicated radio program, a music promotions business and B2B content management and marketing services.

## Promotion

Much of the public awareness of MP3.com has been generated by frequent and high visibility media exposure internationally and locally, in addition to unsolicited third party promotion of the website.

## Brand Values

For the consumer, the MP3.com brand is synonymous with access to the largest legal digital collection of music on the internet and the single location where they can store, manage and listen to their personal music collections through the innovative My.MP3.com virtual locker service. Digital artists and record labels consider MP3.com as an empowerment tool to distribute and promote their music worldwide as well as a vehicle to connect with their fans, gain consumer feedback about their music and access statistics about the popularity and uses of their music. They also view MP3.com as a potential revenue generator, as the company's Payback for Playback program currently sets aside $1 million per month for artists, allocated based on the popularity of their music.

## Future Plans

In order to maintain its leadership in the digital music industry, MP3.com intends to leverage its technology and strategic partnerships with leading websites, broadband application developers, device manufacturers, record labels, software and hardware developers, wireless carriers, retailers and connectivity providers to give consumers worldwide access to their music, whenever they want it, wherever they want it, on any web-enabled device or application. It also intends to provide artists with the greatest potential for promotion and distribution of their music as well as expand the potential commercial application of the company's technology.

The cornerstone of this strategy is MP3.com's newly announced Music Inter-operating System (Music IOS) which is designed to connect various segments of the music industry for the first time. The cornerstone of Music IOS is the new MP3.com Developers Network (MP3DN) which acts as a resource for developers of next-generation products and services designed to enable consumer access to personal music collections from a variety of websites or web-enabled devices.

**www.mp3.com**

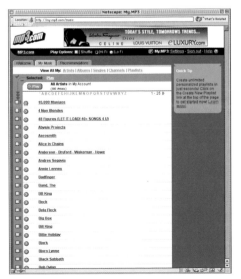

msn.co.uk

## Market Context

The internet is the fastest growing medium ever. Internet companies, have in months, created brand names with greater consumer recognition and perceived business value than bricks and mortar brands have achieved over decades. MSN – Microsoft's consumer internet service – has outstripped even the fastest growth rates in its sector.

## Achievements

With 230 million unique users worldwide and more than eleven million in the UK per month (Source: MSN data), MSN which is available in 33 markets and seventeen languages, has, during its short six year lifetime, established a broader global presence than any other internet company.

Since the last quarter of 2000, MSN has consistently been ranked number one by all three independent measurement agencies in the UK market (MMXI, NetValue and Nielsen).

But perhaps MSN's major achievement has been to create a service that cuts through the dotcom confusion and is meaningful and relevant to people's every day lives. Today, MSN is so much a part of the nation's lifeblood that it has featured in such British institutions as the mass market Coronation Street through to the popular film Bridget Jones.

An unwavering focus on realising the full potential of the internet has also ensured that MSN has staked its claim in the record books on many occasions.

In particular the world of live events has been redefined by the success of a number of seminal world class exclusives on MSN.

In 1998, George Michael chose MSN as the place to give his first interview following his notorious arrest in LA. This set a new precedent. International stars had realised the unique power of internet companies to create an intimate interactive arena in which to communicate directly with fans at the same time as reaching record breaking international audience numbers.

Two years later, in November 2000, MSN made internet history again when it webcast Madonna's much anticipated live gig at Brixton Academy and turned it into the biggest internet concert of all time.

Only 2,800 fans and celebrities were invited, but a record breaking 10.8 million people watched Madonna from their desktops, homes and

from internet cafes. The net magazine claimed that MSN had 'woken surfers up to webcasting for the first time' and 'been a catalyst for change within the industry.' There were a staggering 38,000 online viewers on MSN for every person at Brixton Academy.

The webcast broke MSN's own record for a live event, which had previously been Paul McCartney's return to The Cavern Club, watched by three million people from China to Latin America.

## Key Management

Judy Gibbons, Vice President of MSN Europe, joined Microsoft in 1995 with the vision that 'technology should touch upon and improve all aspects of people's lives'.

She created MSN in the UK from scratch with a skeleton team and within five years turned a paper strategy into a strong business and the number one home internet service in the UK.

Geoff Sutton, Director, MSN UK, is a key player in the success of MSN UK. Geoff has used his understanding of what people want to read about (he was previously Associate News Editor at The Mirror) to bring the most compelling content on the web to MSN.

Geoff became Director of MSN UK in 2000. His aim is to build the best, most useful, and successful network for both users and partners – and a first class revenue organisation.

Gillian Kent, Marketing Director, MSN UK, is responsible for driving consumer traffic and potential business partners to MSN and increasing loyalty and retention by raising awareness of MSN and the service it provides.

Gillian has overseen the evolution of MSN from a Microsoft subsidiary service to a major consumer brand in its own right.

## Background

MSN was launched by Microsoft as its consumer internet offering in 1995. The MSN concept was to bring the best software and content – effectively

**msn.** ™
Make it your home.

*Microsoft*  msn.co.uk

an integrated network of services – to one central place that could be freely and easily accessed by all internet users.

By the end of 1997, in the middle of dotcom fever, MSN was attracting 106,000 users to its site monthly and was starting to provide a serious challenge to competitors Yahoo! and AOL.

As the internet pendulum swung and dotcom fall out hit, MSN bucked the trend to become the first internet site in the UK to attract a million visitors a day (Source: MSN data April 2000) – a staggering 18,000% increase in traffic in just over two years.

MSN has, within the space of five years become a global consumer brand with the recognition, prestige and value of Microsoft's core brands of Office and Windows.

## Product/Service

MSN's easy to navigate site brings internet users best of breed services in the five most popular areas of the web – communications, search, shopping, entertainment and finance.

The combination of MSN's unsurpassed software heritage and its focus on consumer research (it has a group of 'internet pioneers' that feedback on all new products and services) ensures that it consistently delivers the features users find most important and surpasses what everyone else in the market is doing.

MSN Messenger offers free text and voice chat features allowing up to five friends at any one time to have a 'real time conversation' in the virtual world. It is the most used web application in the UK today.

MSN Hotmail is the world's most popular free email service and has over 5.4 million users in the UK alone. Because it is web based, Hotmail users can collect their email free at any time, on any device, anywhere in the world.

MSN Search is the UK's most popular online search service – more used that Yahoo!, Google or Lycos (Source: MMXI). It combines leading edge technology and a team of UK editors to give users relevant, accurate results – fast.

MSN Shopping now brings together the most comprehensive range of goods available in the UK, with over 60,000 products from high street brands Marks & Spencer and Tesco through to internet pioneers Amazon and Expedia. A dedicated shopping search engine, real life 24-hour personal shoppers and detailed product reviews empower consumers to make informed online purchasing decisions.

Money Central is a comprehensive personal finance service designed to help UK users review, understand and manage their financial situation. The service features independent financial information in all key areas of personal finance, from savings to tax. Easy-to-use calculator tools enable users to work out the exact impact of financial changes, for

instance after a Budget.

To offer the best internet content in one place, MSN continually expands its channel offering and now has over twenty themed channels from Entertainment to Health and Women to Sport, so that users can chat with their favourite star, look up a medical condition, play the latest games and be updated on the latest football scores all from one place on the web.

## Promotion

In October 2000, MSN launched its largest ever consumer marketing campaign. Worth US$150 million, the global advertising campaign targeted 'unfulfilled internet users' who were disappointed and frustrated with their online experience.

The campaign centered on the theme of MSN as 'your home on the web'. One of a series of TV advertisements featured individuals in unnatural surroundings in which they looked awkward (eg. a Sumo wrestler in an art gallery) and positioned MSN in contrast as a place where consumers could feel comfortable and in control.

## Brand Values

MSN's philosophy from day one was to combine Microsoft's leading edge technology with the most compelling content and exciting vision for what the internet could be in one central destination.

MSN's aim is to create the most personal and relevant web experience available to give consumers a 'home on the internet' – a central place where they get everything they need from the web and make the most out of their time online.

This 'everyday' web strategy – to make the web indispensable and relevant to 'every person every day' sits with Microsoft's vision of 'empowering people through great software – any time, any place and on any device'

## Future Plans

MSN is working to build web applications (such as MSN Explorer) that work together seamlessly to provide users with complete solutions and the richest possible experience of the internet.

The aim is to create a more personal and relevant web experience – effectively a 'daily life support system' that people do not even have to think about.

Ultimately the aim is to integrate mobile technologies and future platforms so completely into MSN, and user's minds, that they will not even consider which device they are accessing the internet from – experience will be everything.

**www.msn.co.uk**

## Market Context

Free web-based email services have become one of the most important internet innovations. Email is one of the core drivers for internet adoption because people can quickly see the benefits and it is very easy to use. The ability to check email from any internet connection has particular appeal to transient students moving from schools to colleges and then jobs; travellers who want to keep in touch with friends and family on the move; and workers who require a personal account independent of that provided and administered by their employer.

## Achievements

MSN Hotmail has become an indelible part of the internet and one of its most recognisable brands. It is rapidly approaching the enviable position of being a brand name which is synonymous with the service it offers – just like Hoover, Sellotape and Walkman have in their respective market sectors. Just four years after it first appeared on the web, Hotmail became the world's largest free web-based email service provider with over 70 million members, claiming its place in the Guinness Book of Records.

Rapid growth from zero to over 100 million members in just four years – including one year in which the service tripled in size – has been challenging and not without growing pains. Hotmail has navigated this astounding growth well. The initial software architecture put in place by the founders has proved extraordinarily scalable: as capacity grows, Hotmail engineers are easily able to implement additional hardware. While Hotmail has experienced slowdowns and occasional outages – something many sites of its size have had to deal with in the past – Hotmail's problems are usually short lived and affect only a small percentage of its users.

## Key Management

Judy Gibbons, Vice President of MSN Europe, joined Microsoft in 1995 with the simple vision that 'technology should touch upon and improve all aspects of people's lives'.

She created MSN in the UK from scratch and within five years turned the business into the number one home internet service in the UK.

Geoff Sutton became Director in 2001. His aim is to build the best, most useful and successful network for users and a first class revenue organisation.

Gillian Kent, Marketing Director, MSN UK, is responsible

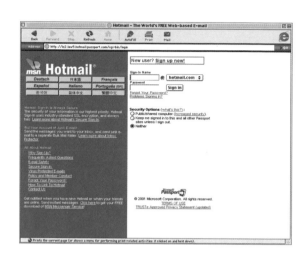

for driving consumer traffic and increasing loyalty and retention by raising awareness of MSN and the service it provides.

## Background

In one calendar year new economy companies experience seven times the life cycle experiences of old economy industries. Nevertheless, for such a well known product, Hotmail has one of the shortest brand histories of any in the world.

On July 4 1996, when the Macarena dance craze was sweeping the planet and Independence Day was packing cinemas, Sabeer Bhatia and Jack Smith quietly changed the web for ever: casually flicking some switches in their tiny Silicon Valley office, they brought Hotmail online for the first time.

Hotmail pioneered the use of the web as a platform for email, winning the support of both internet users and the technology media for its simplicity, features, reliability and speed. Less than eighteen months after the launch Hotmail was acquired by the Microsoft Corporation for US $400 million, becoming MSN Hotmail, part of Microsoft's consumer internet service MSN.

## Product/Service

Hotmail is a free web based email service meaning you can access your email from any internet connected PC, anywhere in the world.

It takes less than a minute to register for a Hotmail account and less than a second to send and receive a Hotmail. Users can have as many accounts as they want, for work or personal use. It does not matter if their circumstances change – for example moving jobs, swapping ISP, buying a new computer or going travelling – a Hotmail account is consistent for life as long as the account is used at least once every 60 days.

When composing emails users of MSN Hotmail can take advantage of rich-text editing to change font size, colour or format, insert links to the web, add emoticons and add their own personalised signature.

In the UK, Hotmail has over 5.5 million registered users and is a fully

integrated part of MSN.co.uk. MSN.co.uk's Communication Centre tells the user how many new messages are in their Hotmail Inbox allowing them to log in, retrieve and send emails direct from the MSN.co.uk homepage.

Hotmail is also fully integrated with MSN Calendar so that reminders can be sent to users' inboxes to alert them to important appointments and with MSN Messenger which enables users to have 'real time' text and voice chat with up to five firends at once. Hotmail users can also subscribe to the Web Courier service which delivers the news, entertainment listings, jobs and travel information direct to their inbox.

Security is a key concern for email users and so MSN Hotmail has recently incorporated a user-friendly Inbox Protector feature which automatically directs spam email messages to a Bulk Mail folder that can be checked separately from the Inbox. Users can also elect to only receive mail from individuals in their own address book or from specified domains to offer an even greater level of protection against unwanted email.

Hotmail has over 100 million users worldwide and is available in over ten languages including – English, French, German, Italian, Japanese, Spanish, Brazilian Potugese, Korean, Chinese and the Nordic tongues.

## Promotion

Hotmail has traditionally not been heavily marketed. There are two historic reasons for this. Firstly, as with many online brands and products, Hotmail's early promotion and adoption occurred almost naturally by word of mouth. In technology, perhaps more than any other sector, the advocacy of 'early adopters' plays a critical role in raising the awareness of a product or service. The fact that users themselves sing the praises of the product is perhaps one of the most powerful factors in the success of Hotmail.

Secondly, in the days when internet penetration in UK households and businesses was still very low, internet brands had little to gain from embarking on expensive mass media advertising campaigns. Hotmail's marketing strategy was focused heavily around online advertising and below-the-line activities such as public relations and direct marketing.

As understanding and awareness of the

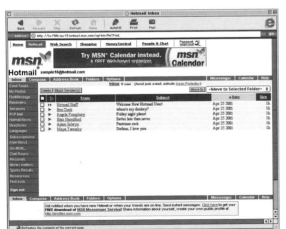

internet – and the size of the online audience – took off in the late 1990s, so Hotmail's promotional activity began to move above the-line. In 1998 an integrated campaign was launched encouraging people to 'be who you want to be with MSN Hotmail'. A national press and outdoor poster advertising campaign was launched, including executions entitled 'Lurve God', featuring a cheesy medallion man who was anything but, and 'Posh & Becks', which showed an aristocrat drinking a bottle of lager.

The following year email became a genuine mass market phenomenon. This was due to factors ranging from its widespread introduction in the workplace to featuring in popular films and books; notably You've Got Mail and Bridget Jones' Diary. A successful PR campaign tapped into both the nations' consciousness and the media's appetite for information surrounding this new form of communication. 'Britain's First Email Diary' was a report analysing 38,000 messages sent over one month by 100 people. The unique and revealing insight into the online lives of everyday Britons received widespread media coverage for Hotmail.

More recently MSN Hotmail teamed up with manners and etiquette experts Debrett's to provide the first definitive guide to e-mail etiquette online after an MSN survey revealed that one in two Britons were looking for formal guidance on what is acceptable when sending email.

Towards the end of 2000, promotional activity targeted two specific groups – job seekers and students.

An online campaign to promote a Hotmail account as the perfect tool for protecting privacy while searching for a new job effectively targeted the growing number of internet recruitment sites. Hotmail went on the road to university freshers' fairs with a direct marketing camaign, encouraging students – an extraordinarily transient group – to sign up for a Hotmail account which would enable them to have a single email address for the rest of their lives.

## Brand Values

Hotmail's core brand values are providing a free, high-quality email service that lets its members access a permanent email address from any computer with an internet connection anywhere in the world. These sit within MSN's 'everyday web' strategy, and Microsoft's vision of offering a wide range of products and services designed to empower people through great software – anytime, any place and on any device.

## Future Plans

Looking to the future, MSN Hotmail will continue to provide the world's largest free web-based email service and continue to increase its user base.

**www.hotmail.com**

**NETBENEFIT**

INTERNET BUSINESS SOLUTIONS

## Market Context

NetBenefit is a dominant player in the European ISP market, providing extensive website hosting, domain name, email and e-commerce services to predominantly the web design and development industry. The UK ISP market has experienced over 1000% growth since January 1996 (Source: NSI 2001) when the internet began to take off in the UK. During this rapid growth period, whilst new market entrants emerged eagerly to grab market share, the NetBenefit brand communicated service quality and the benefits of its established 'one-stop-shop' product portfolio. Despite the market experiencing a boom period in early 2000, which worked in NetBenefit's favour by reducing and consolidating much of the fierce UK competition, the website hosting market is still forecast to grow by 65% between 2000 and 2004 (Source: Magellan Consultants 2001).

## Achievements

NetBenefit was one of the first domain name registrars in the UK and in line with its first-mover status, pioneered an industry leading email forwarding software, MailMapper in early 1997. In August 1999, NetBenefit acquired a French website hosting organisation, Voxpop Internet Publishing, which initiated the Group's physical expansion into Europe. Voxpop is now France's number one website host (source: Le Journal du Net, 2001). Listed

**Today: Bognor**

**Tomorrow: The World**

Domain Names – E-Mail – Hosting – E-Commerce – WAP Services      www.netbenefit.com

on the London Stock Exchange and ISO9002 accredited, NetBenefit then acquired one of its closest competitors, NetNames, in December 1999 to become one of Europe's largest domain name registrars and web hosting organisations. The organisation grew 136% from 1999-2000 and as a result came 22nd in the Deloitte & Touche Fast 50 Technology awards and reached 7th place in the Management Today/Bain e25 rankings in May 2000. NetBenefit has also been nominated for Campaign magazine's Direct Marketing awards for its Cobalt dedicated hosting campaigns, which received a 22% response rate.

## Key Management

Jonathan Robinson, CEO, was educated at the University of Cape Town, South Africa where he gained a BSc in Experimental Physics followed by a PhD in Materials Engineering.

Jonathan started NetBenefit in 1995 as a founder shareholder and company director. He was appointed to the position of Managing Director in June 1997. His full-time appointment enabled NetBenefit's core competencies of technical excellence, constant innovation and depth of expertise to be refined and developed to maximum potential. Following the successful IPO of NetBenefit in May 1999, Jonathan was appointed Chief Executive Officer of NetBenefit plc.

Alison Sparshatt, Finance Director qualified as a chartered accountant with Ernst & Young in London. She subsequently worked alongside Keith Young, founder investor in NetBenefit, on a number of his technology and publishing ventures. She has held several directorships in UK companies, including Finance Director of NetBenefit since its inception in 1995, initially on a part-time basis. On admission to Alternative Investment Market (AIM) in May 1999, Alison became full-time Finance Director of the company, and subsequently prepared the plc to move to the LSE full-list.

Nick Bloomer, Product & Business Development Director, brings to NetBenefit extensive senior-level experience in product marketing, gained whilst working for blue chip companies such as Dell, Compaq and IBM. Nick has vast experience of technologies ranging from broadband through Application Service Provision (ASP) and e-commerce to online communications.

Matt Tidy, Business Manager, began working for NetBenefit from its launch as a credit controller. Matt then moved to Account Management before leading the Channel Sales Division, where he successfully built, maintained and grew the strong base of resellers which remains loyal and growing as NetBenefit's core distribution channel today. As an internet 'Granddaddy' Matt then moved to manage the needs of high-end hosting clients, leading the specialist hosting division before moving to product management. Today, Matt runs the day-to-day business operations of NetBenefit as its General Business Manager.

## Background

NetBenefit was created in 1996 initially as a domain name registration business. At the time when Nominet, the UK's Network Information Centre and domain naming authority was created to control the distribution and ownership of domain names, it was clear that there was an increasing demand for website services. In early 1997, NetBenefit quickly began to offer additional web services to the SME sector and web design community, including self-pioneered email services, web hosting and e-commerce solutions. In 1998 NetBenefit launched its Global Domain Management division which targeted the corporate and legal markets, before acquiring NetNames in late 1999 to increase its global market presence, acquire knowledge and to grow its client base.

Pursuing a European market development strategy, NetBenefit acquired Voxpop in France in 1999, and Voxpop soon became France's leading website hosting company, running its services on NetBenefit's head office infrastructure based in London.

## Product/Service

The core NetBenefit product is based around the purchase of a domain name. The logo 'splash' demonstrates a droplet of water, the initial customer effort, and the subsequent ever-expanding ripple effect that NetBenefit delivers. This includes the setting up of email services, website hosting and in some cases, fully enabling the website for e-commerce, all of which are backed up by the core service – some of Europe's most experienced system administration and technical support services. Innovation has always been a significant part of the brand; as Microsoft launched the NT operating system, NetBenefit began offering an NT hosting service. Indeed, as other products and services have been created, NetBenefit has been quick in creating products to meet demand, e.g. Linux OS, Perl, CGI, ColdFusion and e-commerce products like Actinic and Click 'n' Build.

NetBenefit's core product offering is now led by its shared, dedicated and co-location website hosting

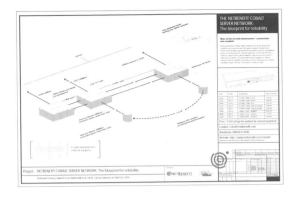

services, with an emphasis on a reliable infrastructural architecture, as customers needs and expectations have developed and matured.

## Promotion

In 1999, there was a surge in domain name registrations and websites grew quickly in numbers. The resulting surge in less experienced and skilled competition led to NetBenefit's highly successful 'Approachable Expertise' campaign which focused on market education and online consultancy. The advertising used a combination of national press, radio, outdoor (billboard and taxi) as well as consumer, business and trade publications.

In mid 1999, clients became more aware of which products and services were right for them. The competitive arena was focusing on 'bigger and better', whereas customers were increasingly aware that they required a tailored service which did not necessarily follow the speed and complexity of technical innovation. Clients began to demand specialist requirements, for example, webspace allowing them to stream video clips, or e-commerce facilities allowing them to process 1000's of credit card transactions via a backend CRM database. This led to more product and service specific advertising with 'need recognition' headlines used in predominantly the trade press. The emphasis was on service uptime and reliability which educated customers identified as critical success factors to their online service.

## Brand Values

NetBenefit signifies technical expertise, reliability, security and superior professional service and support. NetBenefit builds upon its market positioning through ongoing improvement in its customer care and technical infrastructural reliability as flexibility, complexity and uptime become increasingly critical to its clients' internet strategies.

## Future Plans

NetBenefit has an extensive road map of services in development all designed to meet the needs of its core customers and exploit the company mission.

**www.netbenefit.com**

# NetNames<sup>NN</sup>

## Market Context

NetNames is a dominant player in the global domain name management market, providing services to brand owners and their legal and creative advisors that help brands to maximise their online presence. NetNames'

services pivot on the Domain Name as the basic 'DNA' of the internet. The global market for added value services of this kind was worth over US$100 million in 2000 (Source: Magellan Consultants 2001) and is forecast to grow considerably over the coming years. Brands are amongst the most valuable corporate assets of the twenty-first century and the internet brings unprecedented opportunity and threat. NetNames has grown from a registrar of domains to providing more and more added value services to protect brands from degradation and attack from cybersquatters and online piracy. The company specialises in country code domain registration (ccTLD) as well as generic domains (gTLDs – e.g. .com, .net and .org) and has built on this knowledge base to provide an unparalleled level of service and consultancy to clients with global reach. NetNames is an ICANN (Internet Council for Assigned Names and Numbers) accredited registrar and represents the UK on a global stage, competing against specialist service offerings from Register.com, Idnames.com and Snapnames.

## Achievements

Having been established in 1995 as the result of the break up of one of the UK's first web agencies (WebMedia), NetNames grew rapidly in the emerging UK market. The brand quickly established high levels of awareness and became a considerable authority in the UK market. Research carried out in January 2001 placed the brand at the top of an awareness league amongst lawyers and brand professionals in the UK (Source: Magellan 2001). As part of the NetBenefit Group, NetNames regularly features in the Bain e25 technology listing.

## Key Management

John Parcell, Chairman, leads the Board. Formerly a main board director of Reuters Group plc and Chief Executive of Reuters Information, its largest

division. John has a wealth of experience in driving growth at people businesses in a fast-changing, high-tech environment. In particular, he has strength in the development of quality account management to develop sales from a portfolio of high-value corporate clients.

Jonathan Robinson, CEO started NetBenefit in 1995 as a founder shareholder and company director. He was appointed to the position of Managing Director in June 1997. His full-time appointment enabled NetBenefit's core competencies of technical excellence, constant innovation and depth of expertise to be refined and developed to maximum potential. Following the successful IPO of NetBenefit in May 1999, Jonathan was appointed Chief Executive Officer of NetBenefit plc, which incorporates NetNames.

Patrick Van de Vorst, Sales Director Europe, brings to NetNames extensive senior-level experience in sales and marketing gained whilst working for international corporations such as Compu-Mark, Thomson & Thomson, Blondé International Printing and Wang Computers.

David Wood, Group Marketing Director, brings to the group an enormous amount of high-level experience of through-the-line marketing in the B2B and B2C sectors. As Client Services Director of Bates UK, David worked at the highest level on accounts such as The Halifax and Royal Mail.

## Background

The end of WebMedia, one of the first UK web agencies, led to the creation of NetNames in 1995. The company had considerable strengths from the outset by virtue of a memorable brand name itself as well as a highly descriptive name which identified a hitherto unknown service.

Secondly, the company bundled the domain name with three basic services: domain name system, email routing and web direction. These features turned domain name registration from a purely technical need into a customer driven service.

The NetNames team quickly developed a reputation for expertise and service in account handling that the company builds upon today.

In 1998, NetNames US was set up to bring an international perspective to the business and to increase the service being provided to corporates

and significant brand holders, the majority of which were in the US. Research has indicated that half of the global Global Domain Market (GDM) market is headquartered in the US (Source: Magellan 2001).

The diversification to the US coincided with the development of a significant channel for domain name registration services through third party partnerships with portals and web communities with companies like LineOne and MSN. These relationships still thrive and other channel partners such as Dell have also been added.

Initially NetNames' customers were SMEs and private individuals, and included a broad spectrum of early adopters of the internet. In the last two years however, the majority of new clients have been larger corporations seeking more specialised added value offerings.

The general market saw a significant boom in late 1999-early 2000 due to the number of individuals and companies playing catch-up to get on the net and starting new ventures. The cybersquatter reached new peaks of fame and notoriety during this period as more and more names were purchased either to resell or with the intention of extorting money from brand owners.

NetBenefit acquired NetNames in January 2000 and the combined organisation was floated on the LSE in the same month. The merger of previous rivals enabled an integration of web hosting and domain expertise and a greater ability to cross sell.

The group spent a great deal of time and effort through the boom period of 2000 preparing for the inevitable period afterwards when the market calmed and products of genuine efficacy would be sought.

In October 2000, DNRS (domain name registration system) was launched enabling companies and individuals to order their gTLD and ccTLD names from a single web interface and undertake all their internet brand management online. This unique software platform has enabled NetNames to considerably extend its reach amongst brand owners and legal advisors.

## Product/Service

Innovations for 2001 include the launch of BrandAudit, the public launch of I-Watch, I-Search and an enhanced recovery program.

BrandAudit provides a comprehensive search of all domains owned by

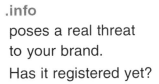

a customer, a full report on domains containing some or all of their name or intellectual property. The audit tool also suggests names that may be valuable to the customer and facilitates purchase. The report is linked to added value services and enables customers to identify if websites are active on URLs owned, and for watch services to be established. The system also enables an analysis of competitor domain profiles.

BrandAudit has been designed as a packaged product to provide a complete desktop solution to controlling domain names on the internet. Recovery services require high levels of human intervention and in order to improve its offering, NetNames have expanded its range of partners in this area.

## Promotion

The strategy pursued is to encourage customers to 'Elevate their Brand' by using the NetNames services.

NetNames believe that to simply promise 'protection' for a brand is insufficient to provide for their client's needs.

The idea of Brand Elevation is being primarily communicated in direct marketing and attendance at conferences and exhibitions. Advertising is highly targeted by using around fifteen publications including Trademark World and The Lawyer. In order to champion its role as sole UK registrar of dot-info, with the new gTLD to be released in the Autumn of 2001, NetNames also promoted the arrival of the new suffix in national newspapers in partnership with Network Solutions Inc.

A key part of NetNames' strategy is in converting the considerable amounts of information collected during the process of registering names all over the globe into knowledge. Once a week, NetNames publish NetNamesNews (N3) Lite, the HTML sister publication of the quarterly N3 magazine, which both reach a circulation of 12,000 subscribers.

## Brand Values

NetNames provide reliable, comprehensive and accurate information to help brands optimise their presence on the internet.

## Future Plans

NetNames have an extensive road map of services in development, all designed to meet the needs of its core customers and exploit the company's mission.

The Group is expanding particularly in growth areas within the EU, and now has an established presence and capability to service clients in France, Italy, Benelux as well as the US and Australia. The development of high-level field sales capability has been another area of investment made in order to pursue the long-term strategic aims of NetNames.

**www.netnames.co.uk**

## Market Context

The uptake of the internet has given more people access to greater streams of publicly communicated information than ever before. In 1999, UK internet usage grew by one third against the previous year (Source: MMXI Europe). Somewhere in the world, a new publication launches on the internet every day.

This creates problems for many people. It is difficult to find, access and manage the required information promptly, easily, and without suffering information overload.

The task of monitoring key internet publications has spiralled out of all proportion. The internet's content is poorly organised, and this can make it difficult for a person to establish what publications are relevant, or even which ones exist.

A person may need to know about articles that are pertinent, within minutes of publication. The information then must be organised into a manageable format to facilitate their quick response.

Through automatic aggregation, categorisation and filtering, NewsNow adds value to the overwhelming volume of online news and information by taking users to information that is relevant and timely.

## Achievements

Thanks to a unique concept and first-mover advantage, NewsNow experienced phenomenal growth despite a shoestring budget and a staff of just two. Within a year of launch its showcase news aggregation site, NewsNow.co.uk, was generating in excess of 1.2 million page impressions per month as well as significant revenues from advertising sales. Being self-sufficient from an early stage was instrumental in making NewsNow.co.uk both a stable ebusiness and a significant leader in online news aggregation.

With NewsNowDirect the company extended the benefits of NewsNow.co.uk to businesses wishing to aid

their website users track the news. Within nine months, 50 clients had signed including Virgin, Sun Microsystems and PricewaterhouseCoopers.

Most recently, NewsNow has brought its technology, research skills and customer service standards directly into the heart of business by monitoring a huge volume of internet information to companies' specific and often unique requirements. This is NewsNow Digital Intelligence. Digital Intelligence has seen the company evolve into a new arena, supplying PR departments and agencies with a personalised press cuttings service for online news. Clients include Toshiba, Cable & Wireless and Ericsson.

In April 2000 the company, then profitable, secured venture funding of £500K from Monticello plc to develop a new technology infrastructure to maximise the company's ability to scale up its product line, customer base and delivery to international markets.

## Key Management

Struan Bartlett, Managing Director, graduated with a first-class honours degree in mathematics, Struan's analytical and creative skills have been key to his success to date. As a technical editor at VNU Business Publications, Struan forged his understanding of the internet industry and its technologies. Subsequently, while working for VNU as a website designer and developer, Struan saw the need for a UK-based online news aggregator. In June 1997, he drew on his fifteen years experience in IT development to set up NewsNow.co.uk.

Nick Gilbert, Business Development Director, first worked as an assistant director and production assistant on the Anglo/French production French

Kiss and the James Bond film Goldeneye. He later made a successful transition to technology journalism working as a staff writer at VNU Business Publications, where he met Struan. Nick left journalism, seeing the opportunity to use

his skills on a start-up internet business, and joined NewsNow Publishing in March 1998.

Adam Newby, Chief Software Architect, graduated from Cambridge University in 1994 with an MA in Computer Science. Since then he has worked in the multimedia and internet industry, including a stint at Autonomy Corporation where he was instrumental in developing some of its leading products. He joined NewsNow.co.uk in autumn 1999, using his impressive IT and management skills to build a successful software development team.

Alex Hazell, Marketing Manager, has been involved in many projects in the last ten years, notably developing the UK's leading hotel and catering evaluation service. Alex's colourful and wide professional experience, particularly within sales and marketing, has contributed to the growth and development of NewsNow.co.uk since spring 1999.

### Background

Founded in September 1997 by journalist and programmer Struan Bartlett, NewsNow.co.uk, the free-to-web showcase site, was launched officially in February 1998. Nine months later, the company launched NewsNowDirect, a B2B service designed to provide continuously updated content from multiple sources to websites, intranets and portals. One year later NewsNow Digital Intelligence was launched, an internet monitoring service aimed at both internal communications departments of large companies and PR agencies.

### Product/Service

NewsNow.co.uk makes headlines from thousands of key news sources in over 600 categories available free to thousands of business and IT professionals. The main top-level categories include information technology, sport, business and finance, current affairs and entertainment. A user can search the 30-day headline archive to find stories on specific topics. Because NewsNow.co.uk updates every five minutes, every time a user returns they are sure to find new articles.

With so many decision-makers such as investors, suppliers and clients finding their information on the internet, crucial deals can succeed or fail on the basis of an impression created by the press. It is vital that every business keeps track of what decision-makers are reading that might affect their behaviour towards the company.

DigitalIntelligence.co.uk monitors the full text of articles from thousands of online news sources for keywords and phrases specific to clients' requirements. These sources include national newspapers, news-stand magazines, trade magazines, newsletters, government information sites, journals and other assorted online news sources.

It delivers intelligence to a personalised account or intranet within minutes of it being posted onto the internet. It also lets clients monitor news about their customers, products, or competitors (both potential and actual), monitor news specific to their industry, and receive direct e-mails alerting them to specific stories relevant to their business.

NewsNowDirect.co.uk is an affordable newswire service for websites and intranets of all sizes. NewsNow's speciality is tailoring news content to the specific requirements of a client's website niche, from ebusiness to Everton FC. Every five minutes, 24 hours a day, NewsNowDirect retrieves the latest headlines from a range of prestigious news sites and inserts them into a clients website or intranet consistent with its look and feel.

### Promotion

NewsNow.co.uk puts its early success down to its flair for innovation with the limited resources it had to hand. Staff asked websites from around the world to include a NewsNow button that linked deep into a specific topic page on NewsNow's site. This helped increase NewsNow's page views from near zero to one million a month within ten months, and in turn increased exposure to and interest in its B2B products.

NewsNow will use e-mail and the post to directly target the people and corporations who will benefit the most from its products. It will also provide seminars for key senior management, publish white papers and maintain a presence at exhibitions.

### Brand Values

NewsNow's success has been largely down to its dedication in providing a quality service. With an emphasis on thorough planning and attention to detail, NewsNow ensures that the client always receives a reliable and innovative service. The company is focussed upon maintaining its promises, of which the most important is to maintain a high level of service. This ensures clients always associate the name NewsNow with efficiency and straightforward down-to-earth functionality. In a recent survey conducted of existing clients, the words fast, dynamic and efficient were the three most popular used by the respondents to describe the company and services.

### Future Plans

The next obvious move for NewsNow is to develop the relatively untouched markets of Europe. Developing news services for European countries is a high priority and the first steps have been made to progress into this market. NewsNow will also establish further facilities to help with the increasing demands from the US and Southern Hemisphere countries. Surrounding these areas of growth will be the continuous development of existing and future products. NewsNow's relentless examination and evaluation of the market will continue to drive its creative solutions to clients' problems.

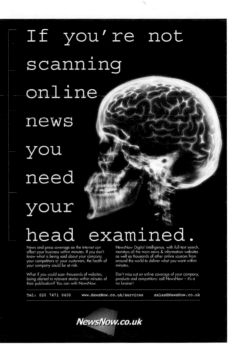

**www.NewsNow.co.uk**

PIPEX®

## Market Context

The internet is moving communications away from traditional formats with websites, e-commerce and email no longer being the preserve of technocrats or corporate multinationals.

Since the creation of PIPEX in 1991, the UK's first commercial ISP, the internet market has grown and changed rapidly. Becoming an increasingly critical tool, vital to companies of varying sizes.

PIPEX focusses on delivering the highest quality internet solutions to businesses and professional consumers, and reinvents itself every six to twelve months, continually innovating and improving the services offered to its customers to maintain its lead in a fiercely competitive market.

## Achievements

PIPEX played an active part in the formation of various key industry bodies such as The Internet Service Providers Association (ISPA), The London Internet Exchange (LINX), and The Internet Watch Foundation (IWF).

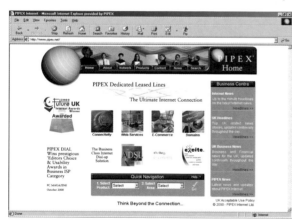

It has won many major industry awards for all aspects of its service, including Best Business ISP in the Future Publishing 2000 awards. PIPEX Dial, has received multiple awards and recognition, once again scooping the top spot in Internet magazine's Best UK ISP monthly survey in February 2001, having rarely been out of the upper reaches of the charts since its inception in 1993. Other awards have included the coveted PC Magazine Editors' Choice Award and Usability Seal of Approval in the magazine's 2000 Business ISP review.

The awards have been the result, in part, of a programme of continual innovation in the UK internet market, bringing PIPEX customers an impressive list of firsts. In 1993, at a time when internet software was unfriendly and difficult to integrate, PIPEX Dial set the standard by developing an easy to install fully integrated software suite. Other innovations were soon to follow including DialSpace, a fully featured web community enabling customers to create and promote their own websites.

PIPEX continued to set the standards and the PIPEX Dial-up network was the first in the UK to offer nationwide connection speeds at 33,600bps and 56k V.90. Furthermore, as the demand for internet security increased, PIPEX was the first ISP in the UK to offer its customers safer internet computing in association with Symantec's Norton AntiVirus™.

## Key Management

David Rickards, Managing Director, is responsible for overseeing and implementing PIPEX's UK strategic direction.

· In 1994 he was appointed to set-up and manage direct sales and customer billing for PIPEX Dial. He was so successful that he was appointed to his current role in 1999 with the mission to further develop the PIPEX brand and services. He has been the driving force in implementing PIPEX's vision of moving 'beyond the connection' and focus on internet solutions that deliver real business benefits, not just technology.

Prior to joining PIPEX, Rickards was Managing Director of a successful direct sales and marketing business. His career spans start-ups and small businesses, giving him an excellent understanding of SME's business needs.

Tom Kermeen, Sales Director, was one of the first employees at PIPEX to help sell the vision of the internet at a time when it was an unknown word in the UK.

In Tom's current position he is responsible for all direct and indirect sales activities, delivering and maintaining significant revenue growth year on year.

Since 1998, Tom has been Customer Services Director at UUNET UK, responsible for all customer-facing post sales activity. Prior to this Tom played a key role in building the PIPEX dial-up business from start-up to servicing hundreds of thousands of users.

Lee Maguire, Product Director, is responsible for managing the full life cycle of PIPEX products from the initial concept through to the final delivery. Maguire's commercial experience in the internet industry coupled with a strong technical understanding provides a critical interface between business and technology.

## Background

Formed in 1991 by internet visionary Peter Dawe, PIPEX was the UK's first commercial ISP. Its service went live with a single 64kbps dedicated connection across the Atlantic. Amongst the first customers were the IBM PC User group and Demon Internet. Now amongst PIPEX's loyal customer base are more than 83 of the Times Top 100 companies.

Set up to deliver high speed, high quality internet access to businesses and professionals, PIPEX led the market, growing rapidly into a multi-million pound business and doubling in size every six months during the mid 1990s. PIPEX also played a crucial part in shaping the development of the internet in the UK.

## Product/Service

PIPEX offers a complete range of internet solutions, all developed by listening to its customers and then striving to exceed their expectations.

Its multi-award winning dial-up service PIPEX Dial is a ready-to-use business/professional solution. A fast and reliable dial-up connection is only a small part of the package, which also includes professional grade web hosting, e-commerce, Norton Anti-Virus 2000 and all the other features a customer would expect from a business-class product. For business travellers a roaming option enables connection to the internet in almost every country in the world.

For businesses with more specialist or demanding applications there are tailored small business solutions (PIPEX Net@Work), a range of web hosting services (PIPEX HostWeb), a web design service (PIPEX Design Agency) and firewall solutions (PIPEX Security). For the larger business, PIPEX can supply its range of PIPELINE leased line services ranging from 64k to 155Mbits. All PIPEX leased lines are supplied with industry leading service level agreements (SLA's) including an impressive 100% service availability guarantee.

## Promotion

PIPEX's early advertising focused on selling the internet as a business proposition rather than selling its own products or services. It realised

that as a fledgling industry, a wider audience needed to be made aware of what the internet was and its benefits if it was to reach its full potential.

The intensive campaign that followed included road shows, visiting many retail outlets throughout the UK, stands at major computer and technology shows and creating many strategic partnerships which all lay the foundations.

A Partnership with the Dixons Stores Group made PIPEX Dial the sole internet access product available throughout PC World, Dixons and Currys retail outlets.

Through its retail channel, PIPEX began promoting the 'Rough Guide to the Internet', a shrink-wrapped box

with a 28-day internet access trial and a specially commissioned jargon-free book created to explain the often complicated world of the internet in plain English. These products proved highly successful and with internet usage increasing, PIPEX began focusing on winning market share, particularly within the business sector.

With the emphasis still on demystifying the internet, PIPEX began an intensive media campaign running through the specialist internet press, computer magazines, commercial radio and in the major broadsheets such as The Times and Daily Telegraph. This campaign focused on dispelling a number of popular misconceptions such as the internet being too slow and that it only appeals to 'net nerds'.

PIPEX's main intention however was to continue the work it had been doing to reinforce the need for UK businesses to get online and to preach the business potential of the internet to entrepreneurs. PIPEX's successful 'Think Beyond the Connection' campaign reinforced the ease of use of PIPEX's solutions, their many benefits to business and professional consumers and their value for money.

It is the strength of the PIPEX Network that is ultimately responsible for PIPEX's overwhelming success with over 50% of new customers joining its services as a result of recommendations from existing users.

## Brand Values

The brand PIPEX is well respected amongst leading industry commentators and IT professionals, having a proven track record for providing leading edge technology without compromising quality, reliability and value for money.

PIPEX has a well-established history of being the leader in its field and the PIPEX name acts as an internet authority in the UK.

PIPEX are redefining the term ISP from Internet Service Provider to Internet Solutions Partner. With its 'Think Beyond the Connection' campaign, it is committed to delivering its customers internet solutions that are easy to use and install as well as being designed specifically for small to medium sized businesses and professionals who appreciate that affordable, mission critical quality and reliability have a value.

## Future Plans

As technology continues to advance, the range of PIPEX solutions will continue to broaden. As broadband (ADSL) and flat rate dial-up connections become generally available, new PIPEX offerings will appear, enabling businesses and professionals to take advantage of the power and flexibility offered by these new connection methods.

**www.pipex.com**

## Market Context

The online film market is a highly competitive one, with major players including The Guardian's Film Unlimited, Ain't it Cool, and Empire. There are hundreds of film sites, although most are relatively small and run by fans, with the majority of the remaining big players owned by large media groups.

The immense popularity of film online is highlighted by the fact that virtually all ISP's feature a film section.

## Achievements

Popcorn was nominated for a Bafta in Journalism in 1999. It came 12th in the dotcom awareness survey by Taylor Nelson Sofres featured in Campaign magazine in April 2001 and was the only film site in the top twenty.

Popcorn was the first site to launch an interactive movie and cinema search with the ability to locate what is on by postcode across the UK. The movie search continues to be one of the most popular areas of the site and has since been emulated by many of Popcorn's competitors. The cinema search is also available through mobile phone text messaging technology.

## Key Management

Duncan Eaton, Marketing and Strategy Director was previously Marketing Director of the Independent. Eaton oversaw the move from separate Carlton internet properties into the umbrella site of Carlton.com in October 2000 following comprehensive commissioned research suggesting that the target market preferred all

HE'S SHORT, BALD AND 72. NATURALLY EVERYBODY IN HOLLYWOOD WANTS TO LEAVE WITH HIM.

TO FIND OUT ALL THE LATEST OSCARS NEWS, VISIT WWW.POPCORN.CO.UK

THE UK'S NUMBER ONE FILM SITE

## WIN AN OSCAR

AFTER SHOW PARTY INVITATION FOR TWO AND FIVE NIGHTS AT A LUXURY LOS ANGELES HOTEL. VISIT WWW.POPCORN.CO.UK

THE UK'S NUMBER ONE FILM SITE

their entertainment needs in one location. Since the move to Carlton.com total traffic for the company has risen 33%.

## Background

Popcorn was launched in November 1998 by Carlton Interactive which is the internet subsidiary of the Carlton Media Group, owner of the ITV franchise for the South East, Central and West Country and HTV.

The aim of the site was to capitalise on the UK's growing interest in all aspects of film and was one the first UK film sites in the market. Now it is the UK's number one film site with over two million page impressions every month.

## Product/Service

Popcorn is a website for movie lovers and offers access to gossip and the latest news from Hollywood. The site features the

## ATTEND AN OSCARS AFTER SHOW PARTY IN HOLLYWOOD. NOT CRICKLEWOOD.

TO WIN TICKETS TO A TOP AFTER SHOW PARTY AND 5 NIGHTS AT A LUXURY LOS ANGELES HOTEL, VISIT WWW.POPCORN.CO.UK

THE UK'S NUMBER ONE FILM SITE

expert opinions of respected film journalists, along with the personal reviews of regular movie-goers as well as offering users the opportunity to quiz their favourite movie stars online.

Popcorn users are kept in touch with a weekly newsletter sent to over 50,000 subscribers.

As well as its film information offering, Popcorn also runs competitions designed to attract users and encourage them to return to the site with 'money can't buy' prizes themed around each film.

It also offers up to the minute movie, DVDs and video news, reviews, star interviews, specialist features, cinema listings and charts as well as opportunities to buy videos and DVDs through its partner WH Smith.

Users are able to search for their local cinemas receiving information about which films are on where and at what time they start with Popcorn's pioneered cinema and movie search function covering the entire UK.

Users can access Popcorn on all platforms from the internet to interactive TV (NTL, Telewest and ONdigital) and it also syndicates content to major portals including MSN, Excite and Freeserve.

## Promotion

To initially raise awareness of the site after its launch, Popcorn used advertising on both TV and print with posters on London Underground in 1999.

Further to this, its promotional strategy has been to drive significant traffic based around mass market film interest. For example, in 2001, it ran a press campaign centred around the Oscars exposing users not just to the Oscars microsite but to other areas of interest on the main Popcorn site. It also ran tactical advertising in the press after the Oscars to promote the fact that it had live feeds direct from the award ceremony itself.

As part of it continuous strategy, Popcorn also mounts press campaigns based around major film releases every month and as well as providing the quotes and reviews for Buena Vista Home Entertainment video releases it sponsors the national daily movie show on Virgin radio, providing the feeds and linking listeners back to its website.

On going sponsorship agreements with partners including Butterkist popcorn and Stella Artois have also been adopted as part of the marketing mix.

## Brand Values

Popcorn aims to be the UK's number one film site. It prides itself on being opinionated and on reviewing films truthfully, even if they are bad. It also prides itself on being easy to use but offering something for everyone. Features on the site concentrate on the accessible blockbuster side of movies rather than the niche areas such as shorts and foreign films.

## Future Plans

Popcorn continues to grow traffic steadily and is currently developing the Trailers section of the site to offer comprehensive access to the top ten US and UK movie trailers.

**www.popcorn.co.uk**

# priceline™

## Market Context

Priceline Europe operates in the online leisure travel sector. More online travel is booked in the UK than any other European country. The UK online travel market is currently valued at £592 million and is expected to grow to more than £3.7 billion by 2005 (Source: Forrester Research 2000).

Any company aiming for a share of the consumer's discretionary time and money is a potential competitor. But Priceline's US patented 'Name Your Own Price' model, as opposed to a fixed price model, means that Priceline is new and different from anything offered to UK consumers by any company.

## Achievements

Priceline piloted the 'Name Your Own Price' concept in the UK in November 2000 and officially launched in January 2001 with a comprehensive marketing campaign.

Since its official launch in January, Priceline has seen visits to the site increase ten-fold and sales increase five fold. The UK launch has been even more successful than the launch of Priceline in the US two years ago, a remarkable achievement set against the current volatility in the dotcom sector.

As part of the launch promotion and sponsorship of the Virgin Radio Breakfast Show, Priceline donated the use of the Priceline cab to the 'Make a Wish Foundation', plus holidays for five people to Disney World and Orlando in Florida.

## Key Management

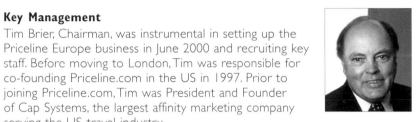

Tim Brier, Chairman, was instrumental in setting up the Priceline Europe business in June 2000 and recruiting key staff. Before moving to London, Tim was responsible for co-founding Priceline.com in the US in 1997. Prior to joining Priceline.com, Tim was President and Founder of Cap Systems, the largest affinity marketing company serving the US travel industry.

Tim has extensive knowledge of both the computer and travel industries. From 1990-1995, he was VP Marketing for Continental Airlines. He has also held senior marketing and planning roles at Pan American World Airways and TWA, including Managing Director in the UK.

Dennis Malamatinas, Chief Executive, joined Priceline Europe in September 2000 from Diageo plc where he was a main board director and CEO of Burger King Corporation. He also serves on the Board of Directors of Reuters plc.

Prior to his role at Burger King Dennis held the position of President of IDV's Asia Pacific region, President & CEO of the Pierre Smirnoff Company and President and CEO of Metaxa Distillers. He also held senior positions with PepsiCo and Procter & Gamble in Europe, the Middle East and Latin America.

Earl Quenzel, Senior Vice-President and Chief Marketing Officer, joined Priceline Europe in July 2000, prior to which Earl held various Marketing Vice-President roles at AT&T. He ran AT&T's consumer loyalty program, True Rewards, during the period that AT&T turned around a ten year share decline. He later served as General Manager for AT&T's $1.7 billion College and Military markets.

Earl also spent more than a decade in the US airline industry — including a succession of senior

marketing posts at TWA, Eastern and Continental Airlines where he built the Onepass program into a frequent flyer powerhouse that was credited with helping save the airline from bankruptcy. He also was one of the founders of the Travel Channel, the 24-hour cable TV network, where he served as the first Senior VP of Marketing and Sales.

## Background

Priceline is one of the biggest e-commerce brands in the US, where over ten million customers have successfully named their own price for travel, cars, telephone and financial services contributing to Priceline becoming a US$1 billion plus turnover business in under three years.

Priceline Europe launched in the UK in January 2001 as an independent company to bring the 'Name Your Own Price' concept to the UK. It is a private company backed by Priceline.com and private equity firm General Atlantic Partners and licenses the business model from Priceline.com. Based in London Priceline Europe employs 50 people at its headquarter site and contracts 30 agents at its customer service centre in Leicester.

## Product/Service

Priceline is all about unsold inventory. It is an e-commerce buying system that puts consumers in control by giving them the opportunity to 'Name Your Own Price' for a range of travel products giving them access to hundreds of thousands of empty airline seats, hotel rooms and hire cars every day.

Backed by the travel industry, Priceline provides a service to both customers wanting excellent savings on travel, and the travel industry wanting to fill empty seats, rooms and cars. Travellers can achieve savings of 20-30% or more if they are prepared to be flexible about the times they travel and the brands they buy.

It is IATA bonded and only works with world-class brands so customers are guaranteed to fly, stay or drive with the best the travel industry offers. Priceline is partnered with many of the leading brand airlines, hotels and car hire companies in Europe.

Priceline operates through its website www.priceline.co.uk or via a free phone number (0800 074 5000). Unlike other websites, it is not a browser site. Priceline is for people who know when they want to travel and at what price. By doing this it can ensure customers do not lose out on seat or room availability. Once a customer names their price and it is accepted, Priceline will book the service immediately.

## Promotion

Priceline Europe launched in the UK in January 2001 with a £10 million consumer awareness and education campaign. The campaign started with national TV advertising around the theme that 'just because you pay less at Priceline, it doesn't mean you get less'.

A comprehensive national radio, press, outdoor and taxi media campaign supported the television campaign.

In addition, there were consumer promotions with displays in railway stations in London, Birmingham and Manchester and a major sponsorship programme with the Virgin Radio Breakfast Show.

## Brand Values

Priceline is a new way of buying that empowers smart consumers to name their own price for airline tickets, hotel rooms and car hire. It helps both the travel industry and people who like to travel by giving consumers the best deals possible on unused capacity, bookable up to 363 days in advance. It is for savvy consumers who are serious about getting a bargain on quality travel.

Priceline's unique business model sets it apart as one of a kind. It has been developed with unique patented technology and is supported by a strong relationship with world-class suppliers, which ensures access to hundreds of thousands of empty airline seats, hotel rooms and hire cars every day.

## Future Plans

Priceline aims to become the biggest e-commerce brand in Europe by providing – world-class travel at bargain prices supported by an unrivalled customer experience.

Following the successful launch in the UK market, Priceline hopes to expand its services to other European markets with Germany as the next planned launch.

**www.priceline.co.uk**

# RealNames<sup>SM</sup>

## Market Context

The internet has been the single most powerful impact on business in the twenty first century. We have seen the success of many entrepreneurial businesses using the global power of the net to achieve things multinationals only dreamed of ten years ago.

As the industry becomes aware of serious limitations with the Domain Name System (DNS) causing increasing confusion with an ever-growing number of Top Level Domains (TLDs) .org, .com, .co.uk, .net, .tv, .infom etc, as well as being impractical for internet-enabled devices, the RealNames Keywords technology is gaining recognition as the leading provider of the next generation internet naming system.

## Achievements

Usage of Keywords is growing rapidly. In December 2000 RealNames served 100 million resolutions (i.e. the delivery of someone to a specific web page using a Keyword) with the total growth over the year as high as 370% and still growing. Because the technology is integrated into the

Let your customers take the direct route to your website

INTERNET KEYWORDS
by RealNames

Internet Explorer browser, RealNames Keywords can be used by 86% of all internet users.

RealNames' most notable achievement is having Keywords integrated into versions 3, 4, 5 and future versions of Microsoft Internet Explorer browser. On the wireless front, its Keywords platform is integrated into Openwave Systems (formerly Phone.com) WAP gateway – the first time it has integrated a third-party service into its gateway.

RealNames has been nominated for several awards including being a finalist for the Smithsonian Awards in the business and related services category.

## Key Management

Keith W Teare, Founder, Chief Executive Officer and Chairman of the Board co-founded RealNames in 1996 with the vision of making navigation on the internet easier using the company's Keywords. Until February 2000 he served as President and previously co-founded and served as Chief Technical Officer at The Easynet Group, an ISP. Prior to that, Teare founded Cybercafe Ltd, owner of the Cyberia brand of cybercafes, and has served on its board of directors since August 1994.

John Tomany, Senior Vice President of Global Registry Services, is responsible for licensing one registry in each country to provide the systems for registering and resolving Keywords worldwide. Previously Tomany oversaw European operations for RealNames, and was also Vice President of Business Development for the European operation. A graduate electronics engineer with an MSc in Management from London Business School, Tomany enjoyed a highly successful career with BT, holding a number of senior management positions after joining in 1987 as Managing Director of Telemap Ltd, a BT subsidiary company. In May 1999, Tomany was appointed General Manager for BT's new Web Hosting & Co-location services, securing a number of major new co-location contracts with companies including Inktomi, Open…. and LineOne before joining RealNames.

Chris Dobbrow, Senior Vice President of Business Development and Sales, joined RealNames in June 2000 in his current role, bringing more than fourteen years of technology publishing and internet experience. Prior to joining the company, he worked most recently as CEO of SmartPlanet, a popular internet education site. Previously, he served as Executive Vice President of Ziff-Davis Publishing, where he helped grow and reinvent Ziff-Davis's leading brands.

David Orren, Senior Vice President of RealNames Global Registrars leads the RealNames Registrars division, responsible for selling Keywords directly to customers in the US, UK, Germany and Japan. Prior to joining RealNames, Orren was Managing Director of Europe for Epicor Software (previously Platinum Software), where he was responsible for all operations of the European, Middle Eastern and African divisions. He was also a regional director for the company in Asia, responsible for direct sales and channel partner management. Orren began his career in the 1980s at Dun & Bradstreet Software, later becoming Managing Director of its Asia office. He has also served as a consultant for such organisations as Mentor_1 Group and MBf.

## Background

RealNames Corporation is a global infrastructure provider of Keywords, a superior web naming and navigation platform that improves on the existing Domain Name System. RealNames was founded in 1996 and is based in Redwood City, California with offices in New York, London, Hamburg, Tokyo and Seoul.

RealNames Keywords were originally branded as 'Internet Keywords' before the advent of the wireless web and other new access devices. RealNames recently re-branded the product as 'Keywords' to incorporate its application across all media and devices, including mobile phones, handheld organisers, TVs or voice access systems and devices. Part of the re-branding strategy was to maintain the consistent use and branding of the Navigation Mark.

The Navigation Mark tells customers they can quickly and easily access a company's website and reinforces that they are at the 'official' destination. It creates a memorable, graphical representation of a perfect match result that catches the eye. It is the aim that the Navigation Mark will soon be perceived as standing for guaranteed navigation to official sites and will be actively sought after by end-users. Because the mark is graphical and shows a mouse hitting a target ('you've found it!'), RealNames expect an increasing number of users to notice it and through trial and experience (as well as RealNames marketing efforts) validate that it represents a quality result.

## Product/Service

RealNames Keywords are a better kind of web address that improves the internet experience. RealNames supplies simple navigation for the net making it easier for users to go exactly where they want on the web from any device and in their local language.

RealNames Keywords can turn a brand name into a web address – without being prefixed with https, colons, forward slashes or wwws. By typing a company, brand or product name into the Microsoft browser line, customers will go straight to a specific web page – even deep within a site.

Often companies find it difficult to monitor the effectiveness of branding campaigns. Keywords enable marketers to track promotions and work out the return on investment on mediums such as TV or radio.

Keywords can also protect brands and customers from cybersquatters and 'typosquatters' who misuse established identities/brands to hijack web users. The non-transferability of Keywords deters the misuse of Keywords and cybersquatting.

Keywords is the only addressing system that is global, allowing people for the first time to navigate directly on

the web in their native language and alphabets. For Japanese, Arabic and non-roman languages in general, this is a huge step forward.

Companies need not go to the considerable cost and effort of registering a web address for every TLD. Instead, they can simply register a single global Keyword to protect their brand worldwide. A single global Keyword can be directed to different URLs in each country.

## Promotion

RealNames' London office opened in early 2000 with the launch held at Internet World in May. The launch campaign proved successful with the Bertha Beans and Slikfone ads which were used in targeted trade press surrounding the event. The UK marketing strategy has been clearly focused on publicity and public relations with one of the company's most successful publicity campaigns on Madonna's adoption of Keywords to protect her web address from cybersquatters. RealNames' events programme has included a selection of top industry events which it has exhibited and spoken at, including Internet World in Glasgow and Paris.

Direct marketing efforts have been targeted at the business industry and have been successful in generating leads.

The marketing strategy for RealNames Corporation in the US has primarily been aimed at raising general awareness of Keywords.

## Brand Values

RealNames aims to make the internet easier and simpler to use through its direct navigation system. Constant innovation and technical expertise are also of great importance, with the combinative effect being customer satisfaction.

## Future Plans

In November 2000 RealNames announced the formation of a Global Registry/Registrar system for selling and distributing Keywords. The model is an open system that locally distributes control and revenue of Keywords and namespaces while encouraging a proliferation of Keyword providers of the internet's next naming standard. The single RealNames Keyword Registry in each country builds a network of Registrars who will develop the full scope of that country's Keyword opportunities and become the vanguard of a better web addressing system. The structure of RealNames Global Registry Services, its Country Registries and Registrars is designed to enable Keywords to reach worldwide ubiquity quickly and efficiently as a next generation naming service.

**↻ Keyword: RealNames**

## Market Context

As websites look to differentiate their offering from the competition, content has been identified as the crucial element in attracting users to a site and convincing them to come back on a regular basis. As website access becomes faster thanks to the advent of broadband technologies, online content is becoming richer, with an increasing number of sites offering streaming audio and video content. This trend is likely to accelerate over the next couple of years as broadband deployment becomes more widespread.

RealNetworks is a pioneer in media delivery on the web. It develops and markets software and services which are designed to enable web users to send and receive audio, video and other rich content. Competition on the software front comes from, among others, Microsoft, with its Media Player technology.

## Achievements

Since the launch of the first RealPlayer in 1995, the company has amassed over 200 million unique registered users. Its user base grows by over 200,000 new users every day.

RealJukebox, released in May 1999, has over 50 million unique users, while RealSystem software is used to deliver content on more than 85% of

all streaming media-enabled web pages. The software is responsible for the delivery of over 350,000 hours of live sports, music, news and entertainment over the internet every week.

The RealNetworks family of software ranks consistently in the top 25 most popular sites on the internet, and in 1999, the company was ranked by PC Magazine as 15th on its list of the 100 most influential companies.

The company has also been successful in migrating some of its user base to a fee-paying model with its GoldPass service, which provides access to premium content in return for a US$9.95 monthly subscription and US$29.99 for the company's premium software. GoldPass has attracted over 200,000 subscribers since its launch in August 2000.

## Key Management

Rob Glaser, Chairman and CEO, worked for Microsoft between 1983 and 1993 before founding RealNetworks. He has a BA and an MA in Economics and a BS in Computer Science from Yale University.

Larry Jacobson, President and Chief Operating Officer, joined RealNetworks in February 2001, having previously served as President and Chief Operating Officer for Ticketmaster Corporation and as President of Fox Television Network. Jacobson holds a BA in Economics with Honours from Harvard College and an MBA from Harvard Business School.

Phillip Barrett, Senior Vice President, Consumer Products, joined RealNetworks in November 1994 after working for twelve years at Microsoft as a Development Group Manager. He holds an AB in Mathematics from Rutgers University and an MS in Computer Sciences from the University of Wisconsin, Madison.

Paul Bialek, Chief Financial Officer and Senior Vice President, Finance and Operations, joined RealNetworks in June 1998, coming to the company from Metapath Software Corporation, where he was CFO and Vice

President of Finance and Operations. He holds a degree in business administration from Seattle University and is a Certified Public Accountant.

## Background

RealNetworks' RealAudio 1.0 audio streaming software made its debut on April 10 1995. By the time RealPlayer 4.0 Beta launched in February 1997, the software had been developed to incorporate streaming video technology in the shape of RealVideo 1.0. On April 6 the same year, RealNetworks put out its first live video broadcast over the web, showing a baseball game between the Cleveland Indians and the Seattle Mariners.

Today, the company's software delivers high-quality audio and video to millions of internet users and with the sport and music deals RealNetworks has struck, it is also becoming a significant aggregator of content.

## Product/Service

The public face of RealNetworks is the free and paid for software it provides to consumers to enable them to enjoy streaming media content. The other side to the company is the B2B arm which strikes deals with websites to use its software and markets content creation and server tools to them.

The company operates a similar business model in both the B2C and B2B spheres. It distributes free basic software to give consumers and businesses a taste of what is possible, then sells more advanced versions of the same software, with added facilities. So while RealPlayer Basic is free, RealPlayer Plus costs US$29.99.

Key releases include RealAudio 8 (October 2000), which delivers CD-quality playback at half the file size of MP3; and iQ 2000 (December 2000) enabling servers to communicate intelligently in a 'peer-to-peer' network, offering increased reliability, as well as the ability to deliver to mass market audiences accessing the web via PC's, mobile devices, set-top boxes and future home appliances.

On the services side, the company has developed a subscription service called GoldPass. For a monthly fee and a one-off charge for the RealPlayer8 enhanced media player, subscribers have access to NBA basketball games, audio and video highlights of Major League Baseball games, ABC News video and concerts from the House of Blues.

## Promotion

The mainstay of RealNetworks promotion has been its product offering. By distributing free versions of its software it has successfully seeded the market, enabling content producers and website operators to start small and scale up, while at the same time ensuring that there would be a market for its streaming media content by offering the software needed to decode it and play it back of consumers.

The success of the model can be seen both in the number of websites using RealNetworks tools to stream rich content (over 85% of all streaming media-enabled pages) and in the number of registered users (over 200 million) on the consumer side.

## Brand Values

The company is widely seen as a pioneer of media streaming on the web. To its millions of registered users, it is a facilitator of cool, rich content and a leading-edge company which constantly refines and develops its offering. With the development of its GoldPass subscription service, its moves to sign content deals, and its themed websites such as LiveConcerts.com and Film.com, the RealNetworks brand is coming to stand not just for software, but for good content too.

## Future Plans

In January 2001, RealNetworks announced a strategic alliance with chipmaker Texas Instruments to develop internet multimedia solutions for next-generation wireless and digital audio devices. The alliance will see RealNetworks' RealPlayer technology incorporated in Texas Instruments' DSP (Digital Signal Processing) chips.

Towards the end of March 2001, the company paid US$20 million for audio rights to Major League Baseball games. Coverage of the games will be offered to RealNetworks GoldPass subscribers. The company is also developing a service where fans could choose their own highlights from a game to watch again one hour after the game finishes.

Also on the subscription front, in April 2001, the company entered into a joint venture with AOL Time Warner, Bertelsmann and EMI, three of the 'Big Five' global record companies, to create a platform for online music subscription services called MusicNet. As a result of the deal, RealNetworks launched a subscription music service in summer 2001.

**www.real.com**

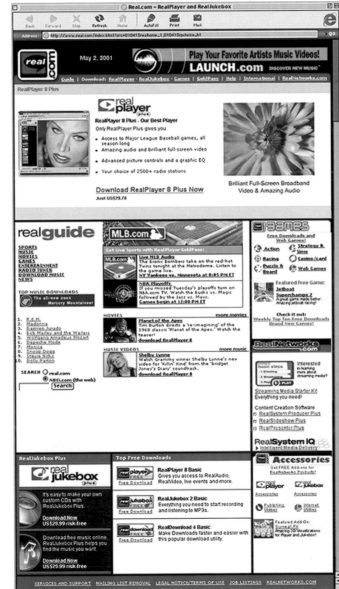

# macromedia
# SHOCKWAVE
# PLAYER

## Market Context

As the technology of the internet improves, it is becoming an ever richer and interactive medium. In the old days, a web page was just that – a page – maybe with a few links. But now, web content has moved beyond the confines of html – the original language of the internet – and into an immersive, multimedia environment. People expect to be able to watch video on the web, listen to music, plays games or view three dimensional, moving graphics. Like TV, the web has moved on from being an information medium to also providing entertainment.

For businesses and brands using the internet as a business tool, it is a competitive necessity to have a website which meets consumer demands. As such, Shockwave plays a vital role in helping sites to develop compelling content which keeps people coming back for more.

Word-of-mouth recommendation is a central ingredient of the 'viral marketing' that many websites rely on, and Shockwave helps to ensure that sites stay top of users' minds. According to Jupiter Communications, 57% of consumer traffic is driven to websites by word-of-mouth.

## Achievements

Shockwave has become the undisputed market leader in delivering media rich, advanced interactive content over the internet. In doing so, it has helped to transform the internet into a fully-fledged entertainment medium, enriching the user experience through enhanced interactivity and a richer visual environment.

Its pre-eminent position in delivering rich media content over the web is reflected in the fact that it is pre-installed on all new PCs and Macintosh computers. Over 165 million users have Shockwave Player installed and approximately 200,000 people install Shockwave Player every day. It has grown phenomenally, with one million installs in January 1999, compared to over five million installs in February 2000. Shockwave Player is now one of the most widely distributed pieces of software on the internet.

## Key Management

Rob Burgess is Chairman and CEO of Macromedia Inc, the company that created and owns Shockwave. Under Burgess' tenure, Macromedia has grown from a CD-Rom based multimedia company into the leader in the web publishing market. Prior to joining Macromedia, Burgess worked extensively in the world of high-performance computer graphics, with experience in key

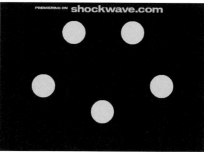

executive posts at Silicon Graphics and Alias Research.

Kevin Lynch is President of Macromedia Products. Lynch joined Macromedia in 1996 and has been instrumental in forming Macromedia's web strategy. Aiming to create practical, powerful, and enjoyable web authoring solutions, he defined and led the development of Dreamweaver, now the market-leading professional HTML editor. As President of Products, Lynch is responsible for developing Macromedia's award-winning family of software and solutions.

Prior to joining Macromedia, Lynch was Director of General Magic's operating system and applications teams, where he pioneered a navigational

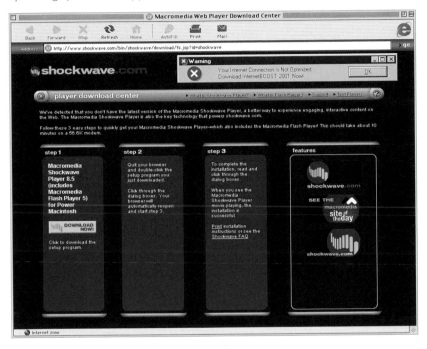

user interface for handheld communicators. Previously, he worked at Frame Technology, where he designed the user interface and developed the first Macintosh release of FrameMaker in 1989, and then led the development of FrameMaker across platforms as manager of Frame's Core Technology Group.

## Background

Macromedia, the company behind Shockwave Player, is a US$250 million software company based in San Francisco with more than 1000 employees. It has been recognised as both a Fortune e-50 and a USA Today e-Business 50 company.

## Product/Service

Shockwave is the web's standard for rich media playback. It is software which expands the facilities that web pages can offer via 'plug ins' allowing users to view and interact with richer content than can normally be created on a web page, such as complex animation, video, audio and other special effects.

Shockwave content can be viewed on the web from within all popular

browsers, including Netscape, Internet Explorer and AOL. The tool for viewing is called Shockwave Player. This is free, easily accessible and, as it is pre-installed on all new PCs and Macintosh computers, widely distributed. Shockwave Player allows developers to produce media-rich content,

which can be viewed on low-bandwidth connections Crucially, it is a system that performs identically on all operating systems and browsers.

Shockwave content is created using software called Macromedia Director. For example Macromedia Director 8, combines graphics, sound, animation, text and video to create streaming, multi-user, interactive web content.

Shockwave.com is another important element of the brand's portfolio. This leading entertainment website is a showcase for what is possible using Shockwave content, featuring pioneering animation, games, music and other creative applications. Shockwave.com offers artists and publishers a powerful distribution model, by partnering with media companies like AOL.

## Promotion

As Shockwave Player is pre-installed in most web browsers and new PCs, it has a ready-made distribution network and marketing platform. It is also in the fortunate and enviable position of being required to view websites that have been designed using Shockwave software. An ever increasing proportion of websites use Shockwave and many lead their visitors to the Macromedia site to download the latest version of it if visitors don't already have it. Macromedia distributes and markets the software through the main Macromedia website as well as through its alliances with key partners, such as Microsoft, Netscape and AOL.

## Brand Values

Shockwave content makes the web come alive. Shockwave's brand is about liberating the user from the limitations of html and allowing them to enjoy a far richer, interactive internet experience. It is therefore a brand with the values of entertainment, empowerment and enjoyment at its core. It is also all about creativity, giving developers the tools to generate the type of exciting and ground-breaking content that drives the internet forward and makes it such an exciting medium.

## Future Plans

Macromedia has recently announced a new version of the Shockwave Player that will take advantage of new developments in the world of 3D animation. Using a powerful combination of Intel 3D software architecture, Macromedia Shockwave will be able to deliver 3D animation to the internet for a wide variety of entertainment and business applications.

**www.macromedia.com**

# silicon.com

**The who, what, when, where and why of ebusiness**

## Market Context

Now more than ever, IT and business decision-makers need to keep up-to-date with the latest technology news affecting their industry. Breaking news such as the Love Bug virus, which dotcoms are going bust and government legislation are key to an organisation's success in today's rapidly evolving climate.

Some printed publications are out of date by the time they hit the newsstand which means that up to the minute, personalised websites play a major part in our lives today.

Rob Lewis, CEO of silicon.com, drawing from his experience of establishing Cromwell Media, identified the web as being critical to the future of media companies.

Launched in July 1998, silicon.com delivers a fully personalised real time news service in both text and broadband TV-on-demand format. Delivered to the desktops of a highly targeted audience of UK based IT, ebusiness and business decision-makers, silicon.com is the dominant player in the UK B2B online advertising marketplace for IT.

## Achievements

Since its launch in the UK, silicon has developed other successful operations in Germany and France, which went live in autumn 2000 and spring 2001 respectively.

The service has become the leading online IT and ebusiness news service in the UK and has a total membership in excess of 300,000, which is more than double that of its 25-plus year old paper-based competitors, Computing and Computer Weekly. It is now the automatic choice for many who need to know what is going on in the world of ebusiness.

In March 2000 Rob Lewis was placed at number six in the Observer's rich list and number seven in the Sunday Times Rich List 2000 and in July of that year, silicon.com was placed at number four in the Sunday Times' e-league. Management Today/Bain & Co placed silicon at number 21 in

its e25 list published in December 2000.

In 1999 silicon.com was the winner of the BT e-commerce Award for Innovation and in 2000 it was awarded for its innovative use of technology at the EEA ebusiness awards. The brand also won the award for best B2B website at the ebusiness awards in addition to being nominated for best commercial success at the Periodical Publishers Association's Interactive Publishing Awards. In 2001, silicon.com was nominated by Revolution for best online property from a media owner.

## Key Management

Rob Lewis, Chief Executive, launched silicon.com in July 1998 as the first online news service that combined text and TV. He previously set up Business & Technology Magazine which he later sold to Felix Dennis of Dennis Publishing. He also set up software development company, Cromwell Media, now InterX Technologies. Rob created silicon.com as he believes the future of B2B media lies in delivering personalised information to its users.

Anna Russell, Marketing Director, joined silicon.com from IBM in 1997 where she was responsible for helping write the business plan that started silicon.com. Anna is part of the management team and currently heads up the marketing function. Throughout 2000, Anna was instrumental in securing further funding and expanding operations into German and France.

Tom Bureau, Commercial Director, joined silicon.com in 1998. Previous roles include Publishing Director at Modern Media (publishers of the Modern Review), Sales Manager at Business & Technology Magazine and Capital Publishing. Tom was also a co-founder of the Connections Group, an internet applications and development company, subsequently acquired by World Telecom plc.

Darren Woolsgrove, Operations Director, joined silicon.com as Financial Director in 1998 having previously been involved in the development of the business plan. Previous roles include Group Financial Controller at InterX plc and as Financial Controller at Kinexus Ltd, a TV production company.

Alan Maynard, Financial Director joined silicon.com as a board director in November 2000. As a chartered accountant, Alan started his career at Arthur Andersen where he spent ten years before joining Principal Finance Group of Nomura International plc. Alan has a range of skills including financial management, strategic planning and mergers and acquisitions experience.

## Background

silicon.com was established by co-founders Rob Lewis and Anna Russell. The news service that combines text and TV is aimed at IT and ebusiness professionals. The company's headquarters, newsroom and internet TV studios are based in Chelsea, London.

The founding investors were private individuals and entrepreneurs such as Peter Ogden, Founder and Chairman of Computacenter and Padraic Fallon, Founder and Chairman of Euromoney. In November 1999, silicon.com raised £11 million from a European consortium followed by an additional £14 million in October 2000.

silicon.com is Europe's next generation B2B broadband publisher and has delivered a powerful and sustainable business model. It produces high quality, independent content from experienced editorial teams based in London, Munich and Paris.

The site is currently receiving an average of four million page impressions per month and has in excess of 300,000 registered users all of whom are senior IT and business decision makers.

silicon.com offers a new era of powerful B2B marketing solutions which are highly targeted, delivering real return on investment to advertisers. Advertisers include Microsoft, Intel and IBM.

## Product/Service

silicon.com is an online news service aimed at IT and ebusiness professionals. It embraced the new proposition – 'The who, what, when, where and why of ebusiness' when the company launched its new look site in September 2000. With more than six new zones each containing five channels, it covers in-depth news and features, analysis and TV interviews with key figures in the industry.

silicon.com prides itself not only on the quantity of users but on the quality of users. 21% of its user base is senior director level.

The service also features a recruitment service (launched January 1999) and has recently launched www.alsojobs.com, a new recruitment service for the permanent and contract IT market.

## Promotion

silicon.com launched its five Ws advertising campaign in May 2000. Going back to the fundamentals of journalism, silicon.com

embraced its new identity, the who, what, where, when and why of ebusiness, to tie in with the launch of its second generation site.

silicon.com's core areas of focus has been to attract new registrations amongst its highly targeted audience, drive traffic to the site, generate high brand awareness and loyalty and position the product as the medium of choice to blue chip advertisers.

Promotional activity includes a mix of telemarketing, direct mail, significant online advertising and promotion and above-the-line activity concentrated in the London and the south east where the majority of its audience is based. The company carefully tracks the return on investment of all marketing spend and the average cost of customer acquisition is £5.50.

From day one, the company has invested a significant amount in PR and built strong relationships with broadcast media such as CNBC and Sky. silicon.com's executives and reporters are called upon regularly as expert commentators in the hi-tech and ebusiness industry.

Significant investment also has been made in forging profitable strategic alliances with other industry players such as the British Computer Society, Yahoo! and MSN. In addition, silicon.com has staff which are dedicated to content distribution ensuring traffic generation to the site and ongoing building of brand awareness.

As part of its loyalty and viral marketing programmes, silicon.com runs regular online competitions, games and promotions. For the launch of the new look site in September 2000, silicon.com developed its very own 'Save the Dot Com' game where the aim was to save the Dot Com Man from imminent demise. The game was designed to raise awareness of the new look silicon.com site to established users as well as attract new users. The game was accessible as a link from the site and as an email file to inspire users to send it virally to friends and colleagues.

## Brand Values

silicon.com presents itself as the automatic choice for anyone who needs to know what is happening in the world of ebusiness. The product offers a personalised, rich content experience which is also intuitive and easy to use.

silicon.com offers a personalisation service to deliver real return on investment to its advertisers.

## Future Plans

silicon.com is rolling out its proven and successful business model into other major markets. The first priority is expansion into Germany and France with the launch of fully localised product offerings – silicon.de and silicon.fr. The company opened its Munich office in November 2000 and the Paris office in January 2001. In the longer term it has plans to launch into other high value markets and produce new products in other market sectors.

**www.silicon.com**

# ● sportal™

## Market Context

The sporting arena was always going to provide the setting for one of the most keenly contested sectors that the early years of the internet would witness. The market for instant sports news, scores, results and rumours has always had an insatiable appetite – from TV, newspapers, radio, premium phone lines and mobile devices, sport receives a great amount of attention and the competition for this market in cyberspace has become equally ferocious.

The internet's unique ability to update audiences instantly has increased this demand.

## Achievements

In July 2000, Sportal was ranked by an independent panel of experts for the Sunday Times/Bathwick Group e-League, as the number one ebusiness in Europe.

The website, euro2000.org, which Sportal produced in six different languages attracted over 129 million page impressions, making it the most visited football website in history.

As well as building out its network, Sportal has invested in cutting edge technology and is working with partners such as Siemens to develop the world's largest football WAP service. Sportal is the only company in the world to provide interactive sports content in multiple languages across every interactive platform – narrowband and broadband internet, both fixed and mobile, wireless, digital cable and digital terrestrial.

## Key Management

Robert Hersov, Chief Executive Officer and Founder, graduated with an MBA from the Harvard Business School. From 1989 to 1991 he worked as a Business Development Executive at News Corp in New York, reporting to Rupert Murdoch. He then became Executive Director of Richemont SA and Head of Morgan Stanley's European media investment banking team before becoming Chief Executive Officer of Telepiu Srl, Italy's leading pay television company. Rob then moved to ENIC plc, the UK-listed leisure and sports company. .

Stephen Nuttall, Head of Sport and UK Managing Director, has an MBA from SDA Bocconi, Milan, and UCLA, Los Angeles and a First Class Degree in Applied Physics from the University of Nottingham. Prior to joining Sportal he was Commercial Director of ENIC Sports from 1995 to 1998 he was Business Development Director of Telepiu Srl with responsibility for international programme rights acquisition and the company's digital satellite platform. Between 1989 and 1993 he worked for Putnam, Hayes & Bartlett Ltd and Lexecon Ltd as a Management Consultant.

Neil MacDonald, Chief Operating Officer, has extensive internet business management experience from BT where he was responsible for BT's internet and multimedia activities in business internet services, the health and education sectors and its ISP activity. Prior to BT he was VP Retail Trading for Fujitsu Computers in Europe, responsible for product development and distribution throughout Europe. From 1989 to 1994 he was Marketing Director (computers and electronics) for Dixons Stores Group and oversaw the acquisition and relaunch of PC World, the leading computer retailer in the UK.

## Background

Sportal was a relatively late entrant into what was a burgeoning but fragmented marketplace. In July 1998 the company entered the fray, both well financed and with a markedly different vision to the competition. Rather than join the headlong rush into launching websites and grabbing

attention, Sportal set about developing its unique technical architecture, which was to be the key to its future as a global brand.

Sportal then forged links with some of the biggest football clubs in the world including Paris St Germain, Juventus FC, AC Milan, AC Parma and Bayern Munich, taking them online. At the same time the company was building its network of offices, firstly in London, followed closely by Milan, Madrid, Paris, Munich, Stockholm, Copenhagen, Melbourne, Cape Town, and Kuala Lumpur.

In the summer of 1999 the world's leading rugby union site, scrum.com joined the Sportal network, combining the interests of Sportal, Scrum and Octagon CSI. The Rugby World Cup of 1999 provided Sportal with the opportunity for its first full service marketing campaign.

Sportal was by then ready to launch as a consumer brand and February 2000 saw the launch of sportal.co.uk, as well as country-specific sites in Italy, Germany and France, followed by Spain, Denmark and Sweden.

## Product/Service

The Sportal network continues to grow with the launch of dedicated country sites in South Africa, (sportal.co.za) Australia (sportal.com.au) and in July 2000 Sportal Asia (sportalasia.com), was launched in English, Chinese, Korean and Arabic, amongst other languages. Sportal has also secured a linking deal with psn.com to take Sportal into Latin America.

Sportal has continually expanded and refined its business model as the market conditions have changed. Sportal now supplies content to MSN, Yahoo!, Excite and many other portals across the globe. The company has also entered into partnerships with a number of broadcasters, creating co-branded online sports environments with brands such as Fox Kids and CNN. 'Sportal on Fox Kids' is planned to be the world's largest online sports destination for youngsters. CNN.sportal.com is the core European sports offer for the CNN.com family of sites and presents Sportal's content directly to a US audience for the first time.

## Promotion

Euro 2000 was the biggest sporting event of 2000 and for Sportal it represented a chance to establish itself as a brand right across Europe. In March of that year Sportal signed a deal to create the official Euro 2000 website. Upon signing the contract Sportal became one of the twelve sponsors of the tournament.

Being a sponsor with this level of investment gave the company high visibility at each and every match of the tournament, which was widely considered to be one of the best, most attacking and most viewed in history. A cumulative TV audience of over seven billion tuned in to watch the action.

Prior to the big Euro 2000 kick-off, Sportal ran a pan-European TV, radio, print and online brand-building campaign. This was also accompanied by an extensive PR campaign across the UK and the continent, featuring the England Head Coach, Kevin Keegan.

After Euro 2000 Sportal continued its association with top class football by becoming the UEFA Champions League sponsor of Juventus FC. With brand awareness well developed, Sportal has concentrated on building on its online community, and delivering value to its users.

## Brand Values

Sportal aims to be the leading global provider of interactive sports content, appealing to both the passion and dedication of the sports fan and also to the inside knowledge of the professional. Sportal's scalable model has a local feel combined with a global reach.

## Future Plans

In the future, Sportal will be further involved in leading edge delivery systems in both broadband and 3G mobile internet, keeping the brand at the cutting edge of global sports media and technology as well as building a brand for the twenty-first century.

**www.sportal.co.uk**

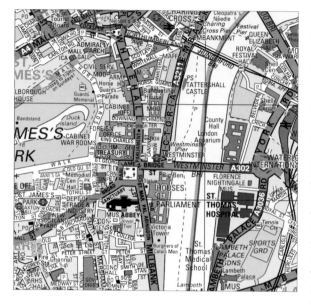

## Market Context

Online mapping has become an active sector as the internet has matured. As people increasingly use the internet to help them with simple, practical tasks – such as finding telephone numbers, looking up train timetables or checking the weather – demand has increased for websites that offer straightforward services of everyday practical use. We all need maps – when we need to get to a meeting, visit friends or tell people how to find us – but we do not always have the right paper map to hand. The internet is perfect for providing this type of information, giving access to more maps than they could ever possess in paper form. It also adds to the ways in which we can use the information, using databases to allow us to search for places by postcode or street name.

In its widest sense, this market for location-based technology has many uses, not only serving the consumer who wants to find an address, but also serving online businesses who want to give location information to their customers. Estate agents are just one group who make significant use of online mapping. In the future, as the internet moves into the mobile arena, the market for location-based technology will expand even further.

## Achievements

Streetmap.co.uk has built itself into the second largest mapping website in Europe, attracting twenty million page impressions per month. The fact that it has done this is all the more notable considering that it has never advertised or received venture capital funding. It is a small company that has achieved widespread recognition on the strength of its product and brand.

It has established a loyal user base, which spans the B2C and B2B market, thereby protecting itself from unpredictable changes in the e-economy.

## Key Management

Streetmap.co.uk was founded by Managing Director, Penny Bamborough. Penny is an IT systems designer and developer who previously worked in the investment banking sector and also for the IT company, Logica. Her expertise in IT and software is at the heart of Streetmap's technical strength and versatility. Her role at Streetmap is primarily technical, looking after the IT backbone of the service.

Kate Sutton is Streetmap's Commercial Director. Kate looks after all advertising and sales enquiries and focuses on building Streetmap as a commercially successful brand. Her background is also in IT, working previously as a developer.

## Background

The idea for Streetmap came when Penny Bamborough was working on an IT project for a dispatch company. The company was looking for a reliable source of maps and Bamborough spotted the potential for publishing maps on the internet. Doing so required some intricate software design, and Bamborough teamed up with her family and friends to develop the software that would enable maps to be published and for people to search them over the internet.

Their success led to Streetmap.co.uk being formed in 1995. The original idea for the service was simply as an 'street map on the net'. A deal with Harper Collins road atlas brand, Bartholomew, supplied Streetmap with the geographical data it needed for its online maps. This was later followed by a deal with Ordnance Survey, which gave Streetmap much wider coverage of the UK.

At first, Streetmap.co.uk was a completely free, consumer focused service with no business footing. In fact Bamborough and her family continued pursuing their own projects after it had been formed. It was not until 1999 that Streetmap started expanding into a commercial business and began expanding

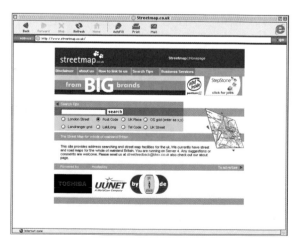

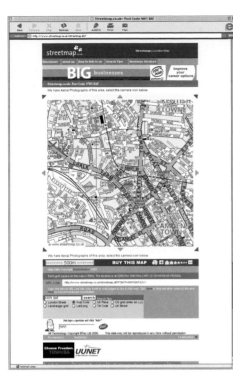

into revenue-generating services, such as supplying embedded maps to other websites.

### Product/Service

The primary function of Streetmap.co.uk remains as an online mapping resource, allowing people to find locations all over the UK by searching with street name, postcode, telephone code, and even latitude and longitude.

Once they have keyed in this data, users can see an intricately detailed map of the area and zoom in or out. An important part of the service is allowing people to insert links of maps into emails or other websites. This enables people to give directions to others, as an electronic 'we are here' tool. As well as showing maps, Streetmap also has a database of aerial photographs, which can also be linked to in emails or from other websites.

Streetmap.co.uk also offers a wide range of B2B services. Just as with the public website, businesses can take advantage of Streetmap's 'linked mapping' service, allowing them to give directions to customers by linking them directly to Streetmap's server.

Businesses can also print maps for their own use from Streetmap's site. For a fee, maps can be downloaded from the web and used in documentation, such as an estate agent's folder or for use by field engineers.

Streetmap's Embedded Mapping service provides map images which can be embedded within a company's own website. Aerial photography

can also be embedded. This is useful for estate agents websites which can show house hunters where the property is on an online map. It can also be used by online directory services and entertainment listings sites.

Streetmap's Store/Venue locator service allows companies to have a search box on their website that allows customers to find the nearest store or venue to them. This is particularly useful for national retail chains.

### Promotion

Although Streetmap.co.uk doesn't advertise, the nature of its service means that it is almost self-promoting. Awareness of the brand spreads virally as individuals and businesses use links to Streetmap's site as a source of maps and location information. Streetmap ensures it is easy to set up links to its site, so that its brand gets spread around the web. However, not all marketing is viral.

Streetmap has also struck deals with several web portals, which use it as their default location-finding service. For example, Virtual Hotels use its maps in its hotel locator. Other promotional alliances include deals with The Independent, which uses Streetmap's maps for its City Guides and Office Angels, which uses its maps on its website. Another important marketing alliance is with Ordnance Survey, which promotes Streetmap.co.uk as a licensed partner whenever it receives requests for online mapping services.

### Brand Values

Streetmap.co.uk is a truly useful service, providing simple and functional information which everybody needs, every day. It empowers people to manage information for themselves and delivers it in an easy-to-use and flexible way. Although it has a valuable commercial offering, Streetmap's brand also has a strong element of public service, making important information available to the general public.

### Future Plans

Streetmap has exciting plans for the future, all of which promise to further raise the profile and reach of the brand. Significantly, it plans to move into providing European maps, expanding beyond its current UK-only base. It is also working on providing US map data, as part of a general shift towards internationalising its service.

Another important area of expansion is in adapting its service for the mobile internet. There is clearly excellent potential for online location-finding services in the mobile personal digital assistant (PDA) and WAP mobile phone arena. Streetmap is already in talks with major software and IT companies to provide a mobile version of the service. An area of particular interest for Streetmap is in using its service on PDAs to provide in-car navigation. The advantage compared to existing navigation systems is that a PDA-based service would be cheaper and more flexible, as the unit could be used for other things outside of the car.

**www.streetmap.co.uk**

## Market Context

Consumers throughout Europe are becoming increasingly aware of health issues and increasingly distrustful of artificial, synthetic health and food products. They are turning in unprecedented numbers to a more natural approach to health and body care. Traditional retail outlets face significant difficulties, both practical and regulatory, in providing consumers with the information they need when looking for a natural solution to a health problem.

ThinkNatural is the UK's leading natural health website. Devoted to natural health and body care, the brand is using the advantages of electronic media to provide searchable and browsable archives of information at the point of purchase, while using traditional mail order and product distribution via the high street to reach the widest possible market. In this way it is contributing to the growth of the natural health market. ThinkNatural is enabling a wider, more mainstream, section of the population to easily learn about and gain access to alternative health products.

## Achievements

ThinkNatural is Europe's leading provider of natural health and body care products. In eighteen months, from a zero base, ThinkNatural has established award-winning websites in both the UK and Germany. It has won widespread acclaim as a leading e-tailer and ranked 11th in The

Sunday Times league of top 100 ebusinesses in Europe. An independent Netpoll survey in the UK found that 92% of visitors to ThinkNatural's website rated their overall impression of the site as either good or extremely good. ThinkNatural also won the New Media Age Effectiveness Award for best health and leisure website in 2000.

ThinkNatural is well funded and has a significant strategic relationship with major retail group, Kingfisher plc (owner of Superdrug), bringing immense reach and strategic benefits. It has

also formed strategic partnerships with several ISPs including AOL, Freeserve, CompuServe and Netscape Online in order to extend consumer reach and brand profile.

ThinkNatural is backed by significant supplier relationships, fulfilment operations and strong marketing campaigns. Mail order catalogues have been successfully launched and marketed. A ThinkNatural own brand range of products has been researched, specified, sourced, manufactured, packaged and has gained high street distribution within a remarkably short period.

## Key Management

Co Directors Carol Dukes and Emma Crowe are both formerly from

Carlton Online and have significant expertise in internet and publishing businesses. Carol originally set up EMAP's internet operations which she then ran for several years before joining Carlton Communications in 1998 to establish Carlton Online, which successfully launched three strongly branded websites: jamba.co.uk, simplyfood.co.uk and popcorn.co.uk.

After launching AOL UK and many other online properties within Associated New Media, Emma joined Carlton Online in 1998 as Business Development Director, running all marketing, advertising, PR, business development and e-commerce elements of the company's three sites. Within six months she had been appointed to the board of the company.

The management team has been strengthened by the recruitment of Dr Mike Hudson (formerly Commercial Director, Healthcare with Nutricia plc), Steve Winetroube (formerly Finance Director with Faith Shoes), Ruth Allen (formerly Publishing Director with EMAP plc) and Steve Clark (formerly Technical Director with Gameplay plc).

## Background

Whilst at Carlton, Carol and Emma recognised an opportunity to use the web in conjunction with mail order to offer an

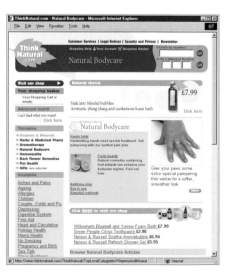

extensive range of the best natural health products, together with the information consumers need when buying them. Thus ThinkNatural was born.

ThinkNatural launched in the UK in November 1999 and fast became Europe's leading online provider of natural health and body care products, retailing vitamins, minerals, herbal supplements, homeopathy and aromatherapy through mail order and via its award-winning website at www.ThinkNatural.com.

ThinkNatural has launched a mail order catalogue that is issued seasonally and is distributed via profiled mailing lists and through the high street outlets of Superdrug.

Original funding came from venture capitalists led by Amadeus Capital Partners. An early investor was David Arculus, ex-Managing Director of EMAP plc and currently chairman of IPC Magazines and Severn Trent Water.

Further funding was raised from the original investors plus Kingfisher plc (parent of Superdrug, B&Q, Comet and Woolworths), Dresdner Kleinwort Benson and several additional venture capital groups. Kingfisher invested £4.5 million for a minority stake and a seat on the board.

## Product/Service

ThinkNatural operates websites and mail order businesses in both the UK and Germany. The core concept behind both of these is to bring together a wide range of high quality products and to provide people with reliable, reputable in-depth information (which is generally not available in shops).

Visitors to ThinkNatural's websites can search for articles on specific conditions, for example insomnia, and the user can then follow links to find the natural health products referred to in the article. Alternatively a visitor who knows what they are looking for can simply search for a product by name, for example, St John's Wort, and go straight to the online shop to make a purchase.

Articles are written by qualified practitioners and specialist journalists, and are supplemented by the contents of three natural health encyclopaedias licensed from Dorling Kindersley. ThinkNatural has made a significant investment in the provision of quality information to its consumers. It is this impressive combination of content and high quality products that distinguishes it from other websites.

Over 5,000 products are available online and the majority are guaranteed to be despatched within one working day. This efficient 24-hour service also applies to products dispatched via the mail order brochure.

## Promotion

ThinkNatural has focussed upon developing a B2C market leading position on and offline, and was one of the first dotcoms to recognise the necessity and potential of a clicks and mortar strategy.

ThinkNatural has invested in creative and consistent

promotion campaigns using both on and offline techniques. Online marketing has maximized customer recruitment through competitions, incentives, promotions and banner adverts. Data capture has been integrated into database marketing activity via the online ThinkNatural newsletter and the offline mail order catalogue. Marketing directed at closely targeted groups has resulted in increased rates of conversion. ThinkNatural's multi-channel internet marketing strategy extended the brand profile online through partnerships with carefully selected sites and the development of strategic alliances.

ThinkNatural launched an advertising campaign throughout the London Underground network and on key poster sites. Adverts in national newspapers and other publications featured the energetic leaping figure of the aptly entitled Rosemary, representing the embodiment of natural health and vitality. The campaign was followed with themed inserts in magazines previously advertised in, and was supported by door-drops. ThinkNatural has also used seasonal, product and ailment specific advertising.

On the high street, ThinkNatural distributes its products and catalogues through Superdrug stores. As part of its multi-channel strategy, a mail order catalogue was launched to extend its reach beyond the internet and widen the potential customer base. A wide range of products, including own label products, is available through its online and mail order channels, further linking ThinkNatural with a traditional retailer and strengthening the brand.

ThinkNatural works with a variety of specialists in order to promote the brand. Fielding & Gibson are responsible for branding, Intiative Media for offline advertising, Flapjack for trade and corporate PR and Yellow Door for consumer PR. The agencies have worked effectively alongside one another to provide a continuous and integrated campaign since the service launched.

## Brand Values

The ThinkNatural name recognises the growing trend towards consumer's interest in natural products. ThinkNatural's tagline of 'the home of natural health' encapsulates its founding members vision of an online, easily accessible shopping service and information source for the growing numbers of consumers who wanted to make alternative choices in the selection of healthcare products.

The company's key brand values reflect an ethical philosophy driven by a commitment of honesty to its customers. This is supported through the provision of detailed information from knowledgeable sources. For example, ThinkNatural use only natural ingredients of the highest quality, and all products have easily accessible, detailed information regarding product suppliers and detailed ingredient listings.

## Future Plans

In 2001 the new German ThinkNatural operation, based in Munich, extended its service offering from a website into mail order catalogues. ThinkNatural products specifically tailored for the German market will be launched.

**www.ThinkNatural.com**

# UK online

UK online

it's for everyone

Protect your family with CHILDCHECK

www.ukonline.net

## Market Context

The world wide web is more competitive than ever before. The internet is big business and everyone wants a part of it. In order to keep up with competition and public demand, new websites are being launched everyday and members of the public have expectations as to what the internet should provide for them. Every website has to live up to and exceed these expectations, which makes it a tough environment. The media is always reporting stories of failure on the world wide web and very little is ever heard of the success stories. UK Online, after six years of steady and consistent growth is one of the success stories.

## Achievements

UK Online was launched at the very beginning of the internet revolution, back in 1994 and is now a well-established UK internet brand. By launching a new advertising campaign that focused on its appeal to everyone, UK Online doubled the number of members that signed up to the service during 2000. Of these new members it attracted a 65% retention rate – a huge achievement for any business.

UK Online was also recommended as a top ISP in the publication Carol Vorderman's Guide to the Internet.

## Key Management

Geoffrey Fenton, Managing Director, has been with the company since its launch in 1995. Since then he has developed UK Online into a highly successful and

popular website, as well as making it a leading ISP. He steered the company through the transition from being a startup funded by Olivetti to a very significant part of the Easynet Group. From the beginning, Geoffrey has been instrumental in making the customer's experience of UK Online as rewarding as possible. He drove the development of the wide range of online information and services available to the UK Online user in addition to being the leading force behind the development of the unique CHILDCHECK service that provides robust filtering of undesirable sites.

Ann Williams joined UK Online as Brand Manager. She develops the brand, looking at new product and service ideas for members and building strategic partnerships. Prior to joining UK Online Ann has worked for NTL, looking at internet product development; The Body Shop, where she gained an understanding of consumer behaviour and the retail sector; and PricewaterhouseCoopers Management Consultancy.

Brad Burton has been responsible for the marketing side of UK Online and was behind the 'it's for everyone' marketing campaign. Previously he worked in the media as a presenter with shows on Channel 4 and Sky television before moving to an independent games retailer, then joined UK Online in 1998.

Greg Raymond, Web Team Leader, is responsible for all aspects of the UK Online website. From day to day he is involved in updating and

maintenance to developing new areas for members. He is always looking for new and exciting ways to use technology whilst maintaining the UK Online philosophy.

## Background

UK Online was founded in 1994 as one of the first UK based ISPs. It has concentrated on providing its members with the best British content that can be found on the net. UK Online was initially distributed through retail outlets such as Tandy and Dixons. In 1996 it was bought by Easynet, a leading B2B internet service supplier to provide the group with a consumer-facing brand and with its backing has gone from strength to strength. UK Online has succeeded where other ISPs have failed because of its strong retention of values. It is not a faceless company and has a policy of personally replying to every member's email. UK Online relies on the excellent reputation of the service it provides to encourage new members to join as well as recommendations from existing members. It employs over 100 people in the Somerset town of Shepton Mallet.

## Product/Service

UK Online provides one of the most reliable dial-up services of the internet

as well as some of the best British content that can be found on the internet. It has web pages dedicated to the latest news, sport, weather and holiday information as well as lifestyle and motoring sections. UK Online was one of the initial ISPs that offered a filtering service to its members. The CHILDCHECK facility can be activated on a

child's account, which bans over 500,000 unsuitable websites, giving parents peace of mind when their children are surfing the net. Web-mail is another service from UK Online that allows its members to collect and send their mails from any internet connected machine in the world.

## Promotion

UK Online's initial major campaigns were focused on being the best family ISP. These campaigns built a loyal following but towards the end of 1999 it recognised that UK Online had something to appeal to everyone and the campaign, 'it's for everyone' was born. Whilst the main family-focused advertisements are no longer running, UK Online has retained its family values and CHILDCHECK is still an important feature for promotion. UK Online has concentrated on exceeding members' expectation by offering a high level of service both in terms of the technology used in the provision of the web and mail services as well as in the call centre. UK Online pursues a viral marketing campaign relying on members' recommendations.

## Brand Values

UK Online is a UK based ISP that tries to capture the essence of the UK with everything it does. The UK provides a rich tapestry with which to work and UK Online provides over 1000 pages of content covering many aspects of life in the UK. It is also an ideal portal for those wishing to discover the UK and for those abroad who wish to stay in touch. UK Online prides itself on being jargon free and provides a jargon buster to demystify the internet.

## Future Plans

It is constantly looking to extend the services it offers to members and is currently looking at online messaging services as well as short message services. It is also developing a shopping service for its members as well as looking at offering members a quality unmetered access service. UK Online are monitoring the market for an improvement in the reliability of high-speed internet connections and when they meet UK Online's exacting quality standards, a service will be developed for members.

**www.ukonline.net**

## Market Context

Internet technology and the expansion of urban living in the past century, have had perhaps the greatest impact on communication and local communities since the invention of the telephone. The sense of membership in the real world is decreasing. Many people no longer communicate with next-door neighbours or take part in local events, and communities are losing their sense of value, need and companionship.

At the same time, however, the internet has created new, virtual communities – in the form of chat rooms and so on. It is catering for individuals who have become physically more isolated and less dependent upon one another yet still crave human contact.

What's more, consumers are coming to understand more and more about the internet market and are taking an increasingly active part within it. Their expectations of this medium have increased accordingly. The pioneers of the new virtual communities must take responsibility for these consumers. Only brands that respect this change in society will stand the test of time.

## Achievements

Since its launch in 1998 the UpMyStreet brand has been instantly recognisable from the use of its vernacular name to the distinct logo. Its focus in becoming available across all platforms distinguishes it from simply being another dotcom. This ability to expand the brand has received positive feedback from the industry and visitors alike.

UpMyStreet has developed into one of the UK's leading multi-platform content publishers. With more than 350,000 unique users a month to its internet site and expectations of over one million users across all platforms, it is perceived as the 'one-stop shop' for local information.

Since its launch, UpMyStreet has won numerous awards and accolades including: Overall winner (platinum award) and Best use of e-commerce (gold award) at the Marketing Direct Intelligence Awards 2000; nominated for a BAFTA interactive award 1999 (factual category); Best use of the Web at the New Media Age Effectiveness Award 1999 and Site of the Year 1999 by Internet Magazine.

In light of the vast number of internet sites available, brand loyalty is essential. UpMyStreet has a loyal audience who are keen to recommend the site. This was confirmed in a recent study with over half of visitors being introduced to UpMyStreet as a direct result from a recommendation (Source: Virtual Surveys October 2000). The same online research also found that more than two-thirds of visitor's opinion of the site was 'excellent/very good' and their likelihood of returning to the site was 91%. These results were significantly higher than established norms, underlining what a valuable service UpMyStreet offers.

## Key Management

Tony Blin-Stoyle, Managing Director, is one of the UK's leading e-commerce evangelists and a co-founder of FT.com. Blin-Stoyle joined UpMyStreet as Managing Director in 1999 and has grown the company from a one-person enterprise to now being one of the UK's leading local information resources. He is a speaker at many high profile conferences and seminars.

Blin-Stoyle rose through advertisement sales for the Financial Times newspaper to become Director of Worldwide Advertising in 1992. He then worked on strategic planning for the FT Group before being appointed Director of Electronic Publishing in 1995.

Blin-Stoyle was a founder of FT Electronic Publishing, which brought together the main units of the FT newspaper electronic publishing and FT Group in February 1998. He has extensive experience in digital publishing, strategic planning and development for online and offline media, worldwide advertising markets and e-commerce.

Mohammed Raja, Head of Marketing and Communications was one of the first to join the UpMyStreet management team, bringing with him six years of local market knowledge. His previous role at Thomson Directories gave him the rare opportunity to work on a Monopolies and Mergers investigation into the classified directories sector, which proved extremely valuable in understanding the dynamics of the local SME markets.

Later promoted to Strategic Market Analyst, Raja was responsible for market development and worked closely on evaluating merits of strategic options. His interest in new media led him to take on the role of Internet Product Manager, responsible for building the ThomWeb brand. Raja successfully launched the ThomWeb business model delivering the product into profit within six months.

Raja, took on the challenge of UpMyStreet in September 1999, working up from Producer to Head of Business Development before taking charge of Marketing.

If you're re-locating, get to know the area like the back of your hand.

## Background

UpMyStreet was built by Aztec Internet and launched on the web in late 1998. The premise was to offer a comprehensive guide to any neighbourhood, using data sets and statistics that could be combined in a user friendly form. By the spring of 1999, the site had achieved more than one million page impressions, largely through word of mouth and a number of positive local and national press reviews including The Times, The Guardian, BBC Online, New Media Age and Revolution to name a few.

That summer, with the investment of family and friends, UpMyStreet launched as a limited company. In December 1999 it signed an equity and content agreement with Open Interactive and the following April it secured £12 million investment from NM Rothschild and News International.

## Product/Service

When UpMyStreet launched in 1998 it was the first local resource guide on the internet specifically driven by the users postcode. It has since developed into one of the UK's leading new media pioneers providing its content across all platforms. Aside from this phenomenal growth in such a short period of time, UpMyStreet prides itself in its commitment to innovation, high standards, content quality and usability of all its multimedia technologies. Its services are already available online, on WAP-enabled mobile phones and on Open Interactive, Sky's digital television service reinforcing its claim – it is not a pure dotcom: it believes that there are great merits in mixing traditional business models with the new to create a sustainable business.

UpMyStreet is not a portal, directory or a search engine: it is a 'real life' guide.

It provides national information, searchable on a local basis, right down to postcode level. By supplying objective, statistically based and consumer-rated guidance to the best

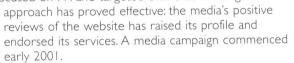

local services and leisure facilities, it aims to inform and empower individuals. The data, which can be viewed graphically and compared against data for other neighbourhoods, includes property prices, MPs, local crime and police force statistics, and local authority performance indicators.

UpMyStreet runs a comprehensive local listings service called 'Find My Nearest…™'. In November 2000 it launched a classified ads service with a number of partner sites, among them Exchange & Mart (ixM), asserta home and Ad Trader, that already exceeds 300,000 advertisements.

## Promotion

Whilst many new media companies have been spending lavish amounts on marketing, UpMyStreet concentrated on research and its proposition and brand, building the foundations to promote the company at a later date. Selective viral marketing and PR campaigns have been the main brand awareness drives highlighting how word of mouth and recommendations have contributed to this success.

Promotion has focused on PR and targeted online advertising. This subtle approach has proved effective: the media's positive reviews of the website has raised its profile and endorsed its services. A media campaign commenced early 2001.

Based on findings from research commissioned to examine visitor habits, expectations and needs, the company redesigned its brand architecture. This has been implemented, strengthening UpMyStreet's core offering and presence. Combined with the brand logo this has created a much stronger visual identity across all its platforms.

Joint marketing initiatives with co-brands including asserta home, ixM, jobchannel.tv and Ad Trader, coupled with increased strategic partnerships with clients including uSwitch have also raised the company profile.

## Brand Values

UpMyStreet aims to inform and empower its users, to enrich their lives by supplying accurate up-to-date information about their neighbourhoods. The services on all of its platforms have been designed to be easy to use.

UpMyStreet continues to build on its proposition by challenging the status quo in providing information at a local level. The company prides itself on its core values of honesty and responsibility through its innovative approach and relevant data.

## Future Plans

UpMyStreet will continue to establish the brand ensuring its relevance and accuracy to all visitors. This will be established over time across all platforms.

**www.upmystreet.com**

## Market Context

Websites generally must be easy to navigate and the quality of the technology must be impressive but not too large to download on a home PC. The range of services must be comprehensive in order to keep customers loyal and encourage repeat visits to the site.

As competition continues to grow, it has also become increasingly important to make the website a 'must see' destination with ISPs and portals needing to keep visitors online as well as within their own domain. Provision of leisure services such as extensive content and entertainment, the opportunity to shop, buy holidays, join auctions and play games has increased as a great majority of leisure activities are now supported in some form on the net.

## Achievements

During February 2001, the Yahoo! network had 184.6 million unique users. It also became the first internet property to reach a unique audience of more then 100 million people. In the final quarter of 2000 Yahoo! announced that through that year the revenues had grown by almost 90%.

In recognition of such an impressive user base and strong business model, Yahoo! has also been rated as the world's 38th most valuable global brand (Source: Interbrand Annual Survey, 2000).

## Key Management

Jerry Yang, Chief Yahoo! and Director is a Taiwanese native raised in California. He co-created the Yahoo! internet navigational guide in April 1994 and co-founded Yahoo! Inc in April 1995. Yang, a leading force in the media industry, has been instrumental in building Yahoo! into one of the world's most highly trafficked websites and one of the internet's most recognised brands. Yang is also on the board of directors and works closely with the company's president and CEO to develop corporate business strategies and guide the future direction of the company.

David Filo, Chief Yahoo!, co-created and co founded the Yahoo! internet navigational guide with Jerry Yang. Filo serves as a key technologist, directing the technical operations behind the company's global network of web properties.

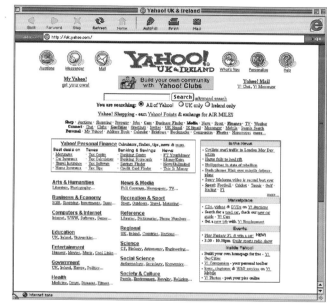

Terry Semel is Chairman and CEO and was previously Chairman and Co-CEO of Warner Bros, spending 24 years helping build the brand into one of the world's largest and most successful media enterprises. Before joining Warner Bros, Terry was President of Walt Disney's Theatrical Distribution Division.

Jeffrey Mallett, President, Chief Operating Officer and Director, joined Yahoo! in 1995 as the executive responsible for establishing, operating and leading Yahoo!'s worldwide organisation. As its President and COO, he is recognised as being instrumental in taking Yahoo! from a start-up to a pre-eminent global communications, commerce and media company.

## Background

Yahoo! was developed by David Filo and Jerry Yang in 1994 as a hobby. They created a list of all interesting websites that they were discovering on the net, thus creating a directory. This became a road map to find useful, interesting or entertaining content on the internet. This site was originally called 'David's and Jerry's guide to the world wide web'. As more and more users, encouraged by the word of mouth, came to the site Jerry's and David's hobby began to take on a life of its own. Eventually the duo decided that they needed a new name for their pet project. At the time, many internet sites began with the letters 'ya' so Jerry and David looked in the dictionary for a suitable name. They found 'Yahoo', an eccentric, fun, wacky race of people in Sullivan's Gulliver's Travels and felt it described their lifestyle as post-graduate students very well. So they added an exclamation mark and a brand was born.

They realised that in order to become an essential part of people's lives, the site would have to develop beyond just directory. One of the early additions was Yahoo! Mail which changed the way that people perceived the brand. Once a consumer had a Yahoo! email account it frequently became part of their daily life.

Following this My Yahoo! was created to enable consumers to personalise their Yahoo! experience by choosing which information they wanted displayed. For example, users can set up their own stock portfolio, choose to display their horoscope or news from the sports team that they support.

Yahoo! community sites were then developed to enable the organic formation of internet communities, while at the same time strengthening the relationship between Yahoo! and its customers.

The company's global web network now includes 24 world sites in twelve languages, with more then 30 offices worldwide with over 40% now coming from outside the US.

www.yahoo.co.uk/gerbil

Day 28

**Weight:** 11g  **Length:** 6.5cm  **Diet:** Seed  YAHOO! UK & IRELAND

## Product/Service

Yahoo! Inc is now a global internet communications, commerce and media company that offers a comprehensive branded network of services to more than 180 million individuals each month worldwide. It also provides online business and enterprise services designed to enhance the productivity and web presence of Yahoo!'s clients. These services include Corporate Yahoo!, a popular customised enterprise portal solution; audio and video streaming; store hosting and management; and website tools and services. The company has formed an extensive network of relationships with an array of ISPs, hardware, software and personal digital assistants, and wireless device providers to make Yahoo! content and services available from any device or access point around the world, at any time.

Yahoo! launched shopping services in the UK and Ireland in 1999. The company's commerce platform includes Yahoo! Shopping, Yahoo! Store, Yahoo! Auctions, Yahoo! Travel and features more than 9,000 retail merchants worldwide. During 1999 Yahoo! also launched a co-branded Yahoo! Visa card with Bank One.

Yahoo! Shops, currently only in the US are physical shops which provide shoppers with a place to relax and can shop online.

## Promotion

The early users of the internet were very much pioneers and brand promotion was limited to word of mouth recommendation. Those who knew and used Yahoo! were given the sense of belonging to a club, encouraging interaction with a brand and given a sense of discovery through the use of the slightly provocative call to action – 'Do You Yahoo!?'

Now an integrated approach has been taken to the marketing mix with advertising, promotions, direct marketing as well as other communication vehicles on the site working alongside PR, co-marketing and educational programmes.

Some of these activities are focused on recruiting new users, but is now moving towards reinforcing the loyalty of existing customers. This is done on

We enable you to maximise efficiency with precise campaign tracking and analysis, and you come back with this:

CLICK HERE **FOR FREE!**

yahoo.co.uk
yahoo.ie

YAHOO! UK & IRELAND

There's a lot more to online marketing than click through rates. For UK clients email us at advertising@uk.yahoo-inc.com and for Irish clients email us at simon@salesonline.ie to find out more.

Follow your team at work. Just be subtle.

Don't let work get in the way. Keep up with the latest scores and watch live video or radio broadcasts of your team. Visit Yahoo! Sport.

yahoo.co.uk/sports

DO YOU YAHOO!?

YAHOO! Sport
UK & IRELAND

a worldwide scale, but focus locally in order to maintain Yahoo!'s human, intimate relationship with its users.

Yahoo! has also developed partnerships with Kmart to launch their BlueLight ISP as well as supporting educational initiatives such as the partnership with Pepsi to launch an integrated on and offline joint promotion driving children to purchase Pepsi and redeem loyalty points accrued on Pepsi merchandise available on the Yahoo! website.

Yahoo! UK & Ireland has signed a deal to sponsor the nightly Channel 5 film for 2001. Appealing to the British love of animals and taking the whole concept of voyeurism TV to the extreme, Yahoo!'s sponsorship idents follow the life of a gerbil called Warren. A daily update appears on TV and he can be viewed on his own website via a live web cam at www.yahoo.co.uk/gerbil 24-hours a day.

## Brand Values

Yahoo! aims to provide a fun and friendly service which is trustworthy, reliable and easy to use. These values have been built using a secure technological platform designed by a human with people in mind.

These brand values are also reflected in the quality of the product that is delivered. Yahoo! endeavour to avoid gimmicks and unnecessary design that could slow download speed and frustrate the end user. Equally, Yahoo! is very careful to control the amount and type of advertising shown to each user. Even with a brand that people connect to emotionally, it knows that its competitors are always just 'one click away'.

## Future Plans

In April 2000 Yahoo! launched its first WAP products in English and German with initial content including email facilities, finance, news, sport and weather. This service will reach consumers in many markets that have limited PC access and poor wired telecommunications. This is particularly true in Southern Europe and is speeding up internet access.

Yahoo! has become the official content provider for Siemens, providing its customers with free access to Yahoo! content. It intends to produce ten different language versions in total from localised sites. With the emergence of WAP enabled phones and other new platforms, such as internet access via TV, usage and penetration of the brand is expected to increase further.

**www.yahoo.co.uk**

## Market Context

Yell.com operates in the highly competitive online directories market. Online directories help consumers find businesses and businesses find each other.

## Achievements

Yell.com is one of the top performing UK sites within the directories sector with a recorded 14.7 million page views in March 2001.

Yell.com features 1.7 million UK classified listings that can be searched by business type, name and location. Yell.com directory search is complemented by content guides for popular search areas such as Property, Leisure and Motoring. These help the user to find the most appropriate supplier(s) by providing advice and additional information.

Yell.com is part of Yell which includes the Yellow Pages and Business Pages directories, Talking Pages and The Business Database.

The famous Yellow Pages directory is used on average 46 times a second, and some 373,000 advertisers place approximately 777,000 advertisements with the company each year. Yellow Pages produces 78 directories across the UK and printed and distributed over 27 million copies in the 2001 financial year.

In September 2000, Yell.com won the Best Business to Consumer Internet Directory Award at the European Association of Directory Publishers Awards in Venice.

2001 is the sixth year of the Yell.com Web awards – the people's choice of the best on the net.

## Key Management

Dr Eddie Cheng is E-Business Evolution Director for Yell.com. He has worked in electronic publishing for over twenty years and in 1998 served as a steering group

member for the DTI's electronic publishing committee.

Nick Harknett, General Manager for Yell.com, is responsible for the strategic and commercial development of Yell.com and was responsible for the successful relaunch of the site in June 2000.

Steve Maller, Chief Technology Officer for Yell.com, joined Yell from MAID in September 2000 with responsibility for product development and service management for new media (internet, mobile phones and digital television).

## Background

Yell is an international directories business that encompasses the Yellow Pages and Business Pages directories, Talking Pages, Yell.com, The Business Database, and Yellow Book in the US.

Yell launched its internet service, Yell.co.uk in 1996, relaunching it as Yell.com in 2000.

The first plank of Yell.com's global expansion came in the 2001 financial year when SME advertisers from Yell's US directory company, Yellow Book, joined the 1.7 million-plus UK businesses which already had a free listing.

## Product/Service

Yell.com gives 1.7 million UK businesses a free online presence through its search database, which is now available via digital television and mobile phones as well as over the internet. For those small businesses wanting to join the online world, Yell.com will create, host and maintain company websites, implement e-commerce solutions and create targeted banner advertising campaigns.

Yell.com Search is structured to be fast and simple to use – Who? What? Where? – with users able to

search by town, postcode or name. Advanced functionality offers fuzzy matching, natural language search, automatic expansion of geographical areas and suggestions based on user criteria – all to ensure an easy user experience.

Consumers can shop online, find out what is on at cinemas and theatres throughout the UK, check the weather anywhere in the world, get travel tips and advice, obtain information about different neighbourhoods in the UK, and even book a holiday.

### Promotion

Yell.com launched its first ever TV advertising campaign on March 1 2001. Using Yell as a verb, featuring music from Elastica, the advertising was based on witty scenarios where people had, or would have, benefited from using Yell.com. The ad used the strapline 'Don't search, just Yell.com.'

To coincide with the campaign, Yell.com introduced an online superstitial

(interactive, non-banner ad) campaign featuring Mr Stick Man. The pop-up superstitials used audio and animation to show Mr Stick Man in different situations, highlighting the breadth of services available on Yell.com.

The series of online teasers was placed on sites relevant to the content of each individual superstitial, as well as on the major search engines Excite, Lycos and Ask Jeeves.

Content partnerships with MSN, Freeserve, Excite and Ask Jeeves reflect the position of Yell.com as a key resource for finding information on suppliers of goods and services. Yell.com has mobile distribution arrangements with, among others, Genie from BT Cellnet and the Mviva portal from Carphone Warehouse. It has also signed digital television agreements with Open….., Telewest and ONdigital's new ONnet service.

While the TV advertising reached business customers and consumers, Yell.com also ran a press campaign targeted specifically at B2B users, which focused on providing information and advice.

### Brand Values

Yell aims to be the best business information bridge between buyers and sellers and the brand values for Yell.com are the same as for all Yell's products and services, namely: trustworthy, comprehensive, credible, warm, straightforward, supportive, confident and 'yellow'.

Teamwork and a progressive outlook ensure an exceptional standard of customer service on a local, national and international level. Yell strives continuously to improve its product portfolio and its level of service to advertisers and customers, while maintaining a socially and environmentally responsible outlook.

### Future Plans

Looking to the future, Yell.com will continue to provide high quality directory services to help consumers find businesses and businesses find each other.

**www.yell.com**

www.zdnet.co.uk

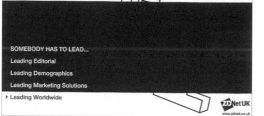

SOMEBODY HAS TO LEAD...
Leading Editorial
Leading Demographics
Leading Marketing Solutions
▸ Leading Worldwide

## Market Context

The one thing that connects everybody who is online is technology – and that is what ZDNet UK is all about. Penetration of internet use in the UK has reached 47% (Source: IDC's consumer survey 2001) with Britain spending 3.5% of GDP on IT (Source: Business Week, March 2000). By 2003, 45% of online users will connect via more than one device (Source: Forrester Research, June 2000).

Technology is the key for progression. The market is changing at a rapid speed and users are seeking up to the minute news about developments in the internet, computing and software industries. Everyone is involved, from IT professionals to gamers to casual surfers.

Research by Forrester in 2000 stated that "Ecommerce revenues worldwide will continue to double each year through to 2001 when e-commerce will represent 8.6% of worldwide sales of goods and services."

## Achievements

Since its launch in March 1996, ZDNet UK has been the UK's leading web destination for people who want to buy, use and learn about technology. ZDNet UK serves an enormous depth and breadth of original, fresh content to a growing audience ranging from IT professionals, e-directors and business decision makers to small businesses and online investors to home computing enthusiasts and gamers.

ZDNet UK is the UK's number one technology website – with 10.3 million page impressions per month and over 1.2 million unique users per month (Source: ABC Electronic Audit March 2000). ZDNet is one of only seven profitable companies on the internet (Source: Standard & Poor's compustat 2000). ZDNet UK had a cumulative yield

for 2000 of £48 and had 209 unique advertisers in 2000 including IBM, BT, Compaq, Carrera and Crucial. ZDNet UK also has partnerships with leading brands such as Kelkoo and AvantGo. The site's users have leading demographics with 70% of users having previously purchased IT-related products or services online in the last year. ZDNet UK reports on a minimum of 30-40 news stories a day and has a high editorial profile, with its experts regularly commentating on both radio and television.

## Key Management

Shobhan Gajjar, Managing Director and Vice President of European Sales has twenty years experience of sales, marketing, publishing and managerial roles in the media business. Gajjar joined Ziff-Davis UK in 1994 and was appointed Group Publishing Director in 1997. At the end of 1998 he began focusing on ZDNet UK and was appointed Managing Director of the company in June 1999. In October 2000, ZDNet merged with CNET to create CNET Networks and in January 2000 Gajjar was promoted to take on the further role of Vice President of European Sales for CNET Networks Europe.

Martin Perry, General Manager, Business was formerly a publisher for Ziff-Davis's flagship print title PC Magazine. His mission as General Manager for ZDNet UK's business unit is to integrate the business information, commerce, community and services into one easy-to-use site, serving the needs of business decision makers.

David Kelly, General Manager, Consumer was formerly publisher for Ziff-Davis UK's Gaming Group. David successfully developed ZDNet's GameSpot UK from infancy to the UK's leading gaming site. The aim of the consumer unit is to become the principle destination for those whose leisure pursuits are centred around the use of technology. While continuing to oversee GameSpot UK, Kelly will also manage the launch of several impending consumer-orientated content and service offerings.

Steve Malone, General Manager, Downloads & Services was a key member of ZDNet UK's launch team in March 1996 and was promoted from Producer to his current role. Steve now focuses on building a range of services that enhances the intrinsic value of ZDNet UK's editorial offering.

## Background

ZDNet UK (www.zdnet.co.uk) launched in March 1996. In October 1997 it launched its gaming channel GameSpot UK (www.gamespot.co.uk) and in November 1998 the shopping channel, NetBuyer (www.netbuyer.co.uk).

GameSpot UK, the games channel on ZDNet UK, qualified as an eBrandLeader in its own right. It is the leading site for UK gamers whatever their platform – PC, PlayStation, PlayStation2, Dreamcast, N64 or Xbox. GameSpot UK's loyal user base consists of over 611,000 unique users per month (Source: ABC Electronic Audit, March 2000) and has pushed its monthly page impressions to over 5.5 million per month (Source: ABC Electronic Audit, March 2000).

NetBuyer is one of the top destinations for users to compare, contrast and buy technology products. With NetBuyer's access to information, users can compare product specifications as well as prices and vendors.

In October 2000, ZDNet merged with CNET to create CNET Networks Inc, creating the global leader in providing technology information and related services to businesses and individuals across multiple platforms including online, wireless devices, television, radio and print. The merger results in a strong synergy and impressive statistics. The company is in the top ten of world wide web property in terms of audience reach (Source: Media Metrix, 2000) and is a top five web property in terms of global footprint. With 24 million monthly unique users and a network of sites in 25 countries in sixteen languages, it is among the top three tech-focused web properties in all major markets. In addition, it is number one in its field in Australia, Canada, France, Germany, Hong Kong, India, Singapore, UK and USA.

## Product/Service

ZDNet UK empowers its readers to get the most out of their investment of time and money in the internet, computing and technology. As such, ZDNet UK has pioneered the channel approach to segregating editorial material from launch – turning each channel into a self-selecting magnet for different types of ZDNet UK user looking for bespoke information appropriate to them and their own distinct technology information needs.

As a long-time market leader, ZDNet UK's mission is to create the best user experience, by leading with the best editorial content. ZDNet UK's goal is to reach more internet users, to continue building loyalty and retention among those users, while providing them with the most valued services.

## Promotion

ZDNet UK believes that successful marketing is rarely the result of one innovative campaign or the use of a single channel. Marketing activities should aim to give the greatest reach and impact possible.

ZDNet UK promotes its brands through online content partnerships which benefit its users, viral marketing, press promotions, PR, exhibition partnerships and mailings as well as advertising in the main trade press.

Its main promotional objectives are to increase brand awareness, drive traffic and increase revenue streams.

## Brand Values

ZDNet UK provides a combination of trusted content, services and commerce to the UK's most active community of technology-orientated professionals and consumers. Built on a strategy combining groundbreaking, interactive technology, with local editorial expertise backed by a worldwide editorial network, ZDNet UK is the leading local source for technology and internet content and commerce.

## Future Plans

2000 was an exciting year with many successes, not least of which was the merger of two leaders of the internet industry to create a true powerhouse on a global basis. Looking forward there are many new opportunities for ZDNet to grow stronger not just as a multinational company, but as a global company sharing skills and experience across all borders.

**www.zdnet.co.uk**

# Directory

**21store.com**
21store.com
Hirst Hall
1 Tower Lane
East Lane Business Park
Wembley
HA9 7NB
www.21store.com

**Amazon**
Amazon.co.uk
Patriot Court
1-9 The Grove
Slough
Berkshire
SL1 1QP
www.amazon.co.uk

**AOL**
AOL
80 Hammersmith Road
London
W14 8UD
www.aol.co.uk

**Ask Jeeves**
Ask Jeeves UK Ltd
53 Parker Street
London
WC2B 5PC
www.ask.co.uk

**Bargainholidays.com**
EMAP Digital Travel
Priory Court
30-32 Farringdon Lane
London
EC1R 3AW
www.bargainholidays.com

**beeb.com**
beeb Ventures Ltd
Room C100
Woodlands
80 Wood Lane
London
W12 0TT
www.beeb.com

**blueyonder**
Telewest Communications plc
Genesis Business Park
Albert Drive
Woking
Surrey
GU21 5RW
www.blueyonder.co.uk

**chello**
chello broadband nv
Boeing avenue 101
1119 PE Schiphol Rijk
The Netherlands
www.chello.com

**ColdFusion**
Allaire Corporation
3000 Hillswood Business Park
Chertsey
Surrey
KT16 0RS
www.macromedia.com

**deal4free.com**
CMC Group plc
Bayley Hall
Queens Road
Hertford
Hertfordshire
SG14 1EN
www.deal4free.com

**eBay.co.uk**
eBay International AG
Unit 6 Dukes Gate
Acton Lane
Chiswick
London
W4 5DX
www.ebay.co.uk

**ebookers**
ebookers plc
Fleetway House
25 Farringdon Street
London
EC4A 4AB
www.ebookers.com

**Egg**
Egg plc
1 Waterhouse Square
142 Holburn Bars
London
EC1N 2ST
www.egg.com

**Excite**
Excite UK Ltd
60 Charlotte Street
London
W1P 2NN
www.excite.co.uk

**Expedia**
Expedia.com Ltd
10 Great Pulteney
London
W1R 3DG
www.expedia.co.uk

**eyestorm**
eyestorm.com Ltd
8 Apollo Studios
Charlton Kings Road
Kentish Town
London
NW5 2SB
www.eyestorm.com

**FinanceWise**
Financial Engineering Ltd
Electronic Publishing Division
Haymarket House
28-29 Haymarket
London
SW1Y 4RX
www.financewise.com

**Flash Player**
Macromedia Inc
Orchard Court
Millennium Way
Bracknell
Berkshire
RG12 1XS
www.macromedia.com

**flutter.com**
flutter.com
Sekforde House
175-179 St John Street
Clerkenwell
London
EC1V 4LW
www.flutter.com

**Genie**
Genie
Nora Building
Herschel Street
Slough
SL1 1XS
www.genie.co.uk

**GoJobsite**
Jobsite UK (Worldwide) Ltd
Langstone Technology Park
Langstone Road
Havant
Hampshire
PO9 1SA
www.gojobsite.com

**interactive investor international**
interactive investor international plc
Holborn Bar
142 Holborn
London
EC1N 2SW
www.iii.co.uk

**Jamba**
Carlton Interactive
3-8 Carburton Street
London
W1P 7DT
www.jamba.co.uk

**Java**
Sun Microsystems
Guillemont Park
Minley Road
Blackwater
Camberley
GU17 9QG
www.java.sun.com

**lastminute.com**
lastminute.com
4 Buckingham Gate
Victoria
London
SW1E 6JP
www.lastmiunte.com

**MapQuest**
MapQuest Europe BV
Soane Point
3-10 Market Place
Reading
Berkshire
RG1 2EG
www.mapquest.co.uk

**marbles™**
HFC Bank plc
North Street
Winkfield
Windsor
Berkshire
SL4 4TD
www.marbles.com

**Moonfruit**
Moonfruit
33-34 Soho Square
London
W1D 6DP
www.moonfruit.com

**Moreover**
Moreover.com
8th Floor
Charter House
2 Farringdon Road
London
EC1M 3HP
www.moreover.com

**MP3.com**
MP3.com Europe
33 St James's Square
London
SW1Y 4JS
www.mp3.com

**MSN**
MSN UK
Microsoft Campus
Thames Valley Park
Reading
RG6 1WG
www.msn.co.uk

**MSN Hotmail**
MSN UK
Microsoft Campus
Thames Valley Park
Reading
RG6 1WG
www.hotmail.com

**NetBenefit**
NetBenefit plc
11 Clerkenwell Green
London
EC1R 0DP
www.netbenefit.com

**NetNames**
NetBenefit plc
11 Clerkenwell Green
London
EC1R 0DP
www.netnames.co.uk

**NewsNow**
NewsNowPublishing Ltd
Frobisher House
89 Lillie Road
London
SW6 1UD
www.NewsNow.co.uk

**PIPEX**
Pipex Internet Ltd
1 Meadway Court
Rutherford Close
Stevenage
Hertfordshire
SG1 2EF
www.pipex.com

**Popcorn**
Carlton Interactive
3-8 Carburton Street
London
W1P 7DT
www.popcorn.co.uk

**Priceline**
Priceline.com Europe Ltd
8 Grafton Street
London
W1S 4EL
www.priceline.co.uk

**RealNames**
RealNames
32 Percy Street
London
W1P 9FG
Keyword: RealNames

**RealPlayer**
RealNetworks Ltd
Ubby Barn
Ubby Green
Chersty
Surrey
KT16 8RF
www.real.com

**Shockwave Player**
Macromedia Inc
Orchard Court
Millennium Way
Bracknell
Berkshire
RG12 1XS
www.macromedia.com

**silicon.com**
NMTV silicon.com
15-19 Britten Street
London
SW3 3TX
www.silicon.com

**Sportal**
Sportal Ltd
40 Parkgate Road
London
SW11 4JH
www.sportal.co.uk

**Streetmap**
BTex Ltd
47 Hartland Avenue
Tattenhoe
Milton Keynes
MK4 3ZT
www.streetmap.co.uk

**ThinkNatural**
ThinkNatural Ltd
Unit 7 River Park
Billet Lane
Berkhampsted
Hertfordshire
HP4 1DP
www.ThinkNatural.com

**UK Online**
UK Online
The Maltings
Charlton Road
Shepton Mallet
Somerset
BA4 5QE
www.ukonline.net

**UpMyStreet**
UpMyStreet.com Ltd
Commonwealth House
1-19 New Oxford Street
London
WC1A 1UP
www.upmystreet.com

**Yahoo!**
Yahoo! UK Ltd
10 Ebury Bridge Road
London
SW1W 8PZ
www.yahoo.co.uk

**Yell.com**
Yell Ltd
Queens Walk
Reading
Berkshire
RG1 7PT
www.yell.com

**ZDNet UK**
ZDNet UK Ltd
CNET Networks Inc
International House
1 St Katherine's Way
London
E1W 1XQ
www.zdnet.co.uk